Praise
101 Days to Ma

In this book there is a quotation ⸻
man which says: "Learning how to be still, to be really still and
let life happen – that stillness becomes a radiance".

I read this book in a day. I found myself unpicking and re-exam-
ining aspects of my life and behaviour. It was provocative and
profound. If I read it and undertook the programme for 101
days, it would almost certainly be profoundly life-changing.

Are you content with your present? Are you content with what
you perceive to be your future? If so, do not read this book: no
need. If not, undertaking the programme over 101 days would
help you clarify, at a level you perhaps have never done before,
how you want to live and to be.

The programme requires commitment. Imagine yourself doing
a twelve week summer school or training for the London Mara-
thon. In a systematic way you are going to need to devote time
and energy to it each day. So, before you start, make some decisions about what you may have to 'cut out' for that period. The
programme also requires courage. Almost all, if not all, of us
need a support mechanism in our lives. Tell your close friends
and family that you are undertaking this course. They can offer
you encouragement along the way: be your programme buddies.

This book is a tool. It is both a car and a bit of a navigator for the
journey. You are the driver, ultimately deciding the nature of
the journey through listening to your own inner compass. Each
person who undertakes this programme will find themselves at
the end at a destination that is unique and particular to them.
The programme can help you to more clearly understand who
you are and, specifically, what makes you happy. In your own
particular way it can help you learn to be really still, let life

happen, and enjoy every part of its rollercoaster ride. Ultimately, I think you may find the journey itself is the destination.

Dr. Raphael Jay Adjani F.R.S.A. Director, Center for Creative Development and academic at Goldsmiths, University of London

I have always found Roy's approach to change inspiring and thought-provoking. His collaboration in this book made it a must try for me and I wasn't disappointed. I'd recommend it if you want something different in your work or personal life but don't know where to start – the answer as you will quickly see, is always "with yourself"!!!

Dawn Caswell, Human Alchemy, specialist in Transformational Management Team Development

A great resource with some innovative ideas and perfect for dipping into for some daily inspiration. I especially liked the idea of keeping a 'Mood diary' and it's helpful that there is space for notes at the end of each day's exercise. The quotations peppered throughout were thought-provoking too.

Janey Lee Grace – author of *Imperfectly Natural Woman*

101 days to Make a Change – a book? No. It's more than that. This is our personal MOT manual exploring every part of our lives. It's not a book just to read, it's a brilliant manual with practical and profound exercises to complete so that we can live at our best and give our best. It's brilliant – it's to be used every year – and I highly recommend it.

Lindsey Reed, FInstLM, LCH Dip; Master NLP Practitioner, licensed career coach and confidence coach

Having led transformational change in busy, large and complex organisations most of my adult life, I struggle to find a book on personal development that inspires me to read it from cover to cover, never mind putting it into practice. Well. This did both!

Paul Barron, CBE, retired Chief Executive of National Air Traffic Services and now freelance business advisor and mentor

The authors invite us on a journey of personal growth and self-discovery. They offer practical down to earth support full of possibility and based upon sound reasoning. This book will really help you to transform your life if you let it allowing you to reach your goals both personal and professional. It is a tool for change at the deepest level.

Terri Broughton, Master Practitioner and Trainer of NLP, Director of Teaching and Learning Development at Kings Lynn Academy

101 Days to Make a Change

Daily Strategies to Move from Knowing to Being

Roy Leighton, Emma Kilbey and Kristina Bill

Crown House Publishing Ltd
www.crownhouse.co.uk
www.crownhousepublishing.com

First published by

Crown House Publishing Ltd
Crown Buildings, Bancyfelin, Carmarthen, Wales, SA33 5ND, UK
www.crownhouse.co.uk

and

Crown House Publishing Company LLC
6 Trowbridge Drive, Suite 5, Bethel, CT 06801, USA
www.crownhousepublishing.com

British Library Cataloguing-in-Publication Data
A catalogue entry for this book is available
from the British Library.

Print ISBN 978-184590678-8
Mobi ISBN 978-184590767-9
ePub ISBN 978-184590768-6
LCCN 2010937287

Printed and bound in the UK by
Bell & Bain Ltd., Glasgow

Roy would like to dedicate this book to
Ben Frow for getting him on the path for which
he will always be grateful

Emma would like to dedicate this book
to Greg, Flo and Lynn

Kristina would like to dedicate this book
to John Akayzar

Contents

Introduction

Thank you for picking up this book. We hope it will be of some use to you for the next 101 days and beyond. The minimum it will do is to give you food for thought, but if you apply yourself to the exercises suggested it might just change your life ...

Don't be put off by that outrageous claim. To suggest that a book may be life changing, particularly by the authors, may seem arrogant! But we know that our view is based on sound reasoning and empirical evidence. The years we have spent developing the exercises in this book and refining the thinking behind them, as well as seeing the tangible results of applying them, make us confident in our claim. It's important to understand that this book has been designed with the primary purpose of building confidence, resilience and happiness in the reader. It would negate much of what we are suggesting if we were unable to put it into practice ourselves.

The underlying system that supports the journey of personal growth used in our work as a consultancy is based on the work of Dr Clare W. Graves. His ideas and research around the development of the mature and happy adult are adhered to in the progression of the 101 days. Graves came up with a model that charts and identifies the development of adult maturity via different stages of being. These phases are identified by our values and drives, which then dictate the way we see the world and how we relate to others. As each stage moves onto the next, it transcends but includes the previous one. As Graves said:

> [W]hat I am proposing is that the psychology of the mature human being is an unfolding, emergent, oscillating, spiralling process marked by progressive subordination of older, lower-order behaviour systems to newer, higher-order systems as man's existential problems change. These systems alternate between focus upon the external world, and attempts to change it, and focus upon the inner world, and attempts to come to peace with it. (1971)

One thing that we can definitely rely on in life is change – whether it's an internal shift or an external event that demands we adapt. Graves emphasised that if a person's world changes they must adjust their thinking or behaviour, and vice versa. Effectively managing this constant problem-based reality is what drives the development of children to become healthy, balanced adults, and assists us all in reflecting on our own evolution. When we desire to keep things as they are, and not engage with the dynamic and ever-changing reality of evolution, we jeopardise the effectiveness and happiness of individuals and organisations.

A summary of the Gravesian levels of human existence is set out in the table below. The table reads from bottom to top.

World view	Level of human existence	Thinking/behaviour
All things are dependent on each other for survival	Holistic	Global, holistic
The world is complex	Complexity	Systems thinking, analysis
We are all equal	Community	Empathy, collaboration
Full of opportunities	Enterprise	Working for personal reward in the medium and long term
The world is in chaos	Order	Hierarchy, rules, structure
Only the strong survive	Self	Impulsive, power, instant gain
Unsafe, mysterious, unknown forces around us	Tribal	Family, icons, rituals, safety
No world view at this level	Survival	Eat, sleep, sex

Source: Bowkett et al., 2008

When all levels are healthy and open, then individuals – and the organisations they may be part of – share not only a vision but have a model for dialogue and understanding, which leads to progress. When any individual, organisation or culture becomes fixed and closed at one level, conflict will inevitably be generated by this suppression of the natural process of evolution. The question is not so much 'Where am I?' but rather 'Am I open or closed?' to each level.

To return to Graves:

> I am not saying in this conception of adult behaviour that one style of being, one form of human existence is inevitably and in all circumstances superior to or better than another form of human existence, another style of being. What I am saying is that when one form of being is more congruent with the realities of existence, then it is the better form of living for those realities. (1971)

We hope that through the clear stages of development shown in this book you will be inspired to give energy and life-force to those around you as you grow in determination, confidence, competence and compassion.

How to approach this book

The book is broken down into eight sections which correspond to Graves's levels of human existence. Within this structure each of the 101 days follows the same format: quote, text and exercise or question. There are two ways to approach it. The first is to follow the days in order. The second is just to dip into the book randomly whenever you get the urge. Both will be of use, but moving systematically through the levels, without skipping sections or running out of sequence, is the ideal option. The choice is yours.

The exercises vary in length; some are one-offs while others can be repeated – either for the remainder of the section or the duration of the book (and beyond). 'Today's exercise' is the one we suggest you do on that day. At the end of each day there is also a reminder of the exercises that we suggest you keep doing throughout the thirteen days of that particular section, as well as the ones we recommend you keep up throughout the entire 101-day process. There is also space for notes. Again, the choice is yours as to how many of these exercises you do.

We have enjoyed the challenge of writing this book and hope that you find it a practical resource to help you on your travels. Wherever you are on your particular and very personal path, it's always important to take some time to check out not just your direction but your reason for heading that way in the first place.

May your journey be surprising and rewarding – and we sincerely hope that these words are fuel for it!

Section 1

Survival

Getting the Basics Right

Are You Waving or Drowning?

Day 1

Begin and end with gratitude

You don't have to see the whole staircase –
just take the first step.

Martin Luther King

Perhaps the most fundamental element to get right in life is our ability to experience love and feel gratitude, so it seems appropriate to start right there. Why is gratitude so important? Feeling grateful for all that we are and have is deeply satisfying and enriching. It also reduces feelings such as inadequacy, envy and frustration which are the usual stumbling blocks to reaching our full potential. Plus it aids acceptance of other people and their situations, and thereby creates greater empathy.

We will introduce a simple but effective exercise that is designed to top and tail each day. This exercise will, over time, reduce negative thoughts, aid clarity, increase a sense of contentment and lead to greater inner peace.

Today's exercise

Wake up with gratitude

Take a few moments, just as you wake up, to immediately 'catch your mind' and think about a person, a place, a song or an activity that you love. Stay with the thought, elaborate on the visualisation and really go into it until you experience a sensation of love; then set your intention to go into your day with that loving feeling. It may not last all day but the fact that you did it first thing becomes a habit and has an accumulative effect.

It is also important to round up the day's events and experiences and to clear your mind for that all-important sleep to have its full regenerative effect. Before going to sleep, lie down flat on your back and relax (in bed or on the floor). Gently rest your hands by your side or on your chest, whichever feels right. Now start to run a list in your head of all the things you are grateful for. Start with yourself, including your body, mind, soul, achievements and so on. Move on to all your relationships, experiences, comforts and joys. Imagine that you gently hold all this gratitude in your heart and set your intention to wake up the next day and be even more grateful for all your gifts.

Notes:

Day 2

Wake up your body

A healthy mind in a healthy body.

Buddhist proverb

We all know that it's advisable to look after our bodies, yet it can seem impossible to prioritise the time and the space needed to do so. If we eat unhealthily and refrain from exercising or taking adequate rest there is a risk of a build-up of toxins in the system. In time this can lead to disease. Traditional Western ideas, both scientific and religious, have in some ways led to the belief of a separation between the physical body and mental and emotional activities. This can make it difficult to appreciate to what extent general mental and emotional health can impact the physical body, and vice versa.

The body is full of sensory centres that make it possible for us to experience feelings of love, contentment, ecstasy, pain and so on. Toxins left in the body can start to consume vital energy and clog the system. When our energy is low we may become less focused, attentive, open-minded or thoughtful – less aware of and in touch with our feelings. Furthermore, various additives in foods can create chemical imbalances in the body so that physical ailments as well as mood swings and depressive symptoms may ensue. The more toxins are eliminated, the greater our ability to feel energised, alert and relaxed.

As well as causing harm by neglecting our bodies physically, maintaining a negative body image can also be very destructive. This may stem from a variety of sources, such as pressure from popular culture, religious beliefs, traumatic personal experience and so on. An essential element of personal development is to fully accept who we are. A negative body image equates to a lack of self-acceptance which can hinder personal growth. These are extremely personal topics and can be very deep-seated.

The process of investigation and the consequent discovering and demystifying of those beliefs can be painful but ultimately hugely freeing and rewarding.

Exercise and eating diary

Do you accept the mind–body connection or are you rejecting it? If so, why? What are your reservations or fears? What is your body image? Are you dragging around negative ideas about your body? How can you celebrate and be grateful for the health and the body that you have?

Starting today, keep a food and exercise journal for the next ten days. Where are your blind spots? Are you getting adequate rest or are you always doing something? Do you eat a lot of junk food that is potentially clogging your system?

Commit to changing at least one bad habit regarding your diet, exercise and rest. Commit to working on gratitude for your body and an improved body image.

Notes:

Exercises throughout this section ◇   Exercises throughout the book
Exercise and eating diary   Wake up with gratitude

Day 3

Knowing a habit when you see one

Failure is an attitude, not an outcome.

Harvey Mackay

How do we recognise our habits? How do we determine if they are good or bad? Habits are repetitive behavioural patterns that can be useful if they cut the delivery time of a certain positive result, or they can be negative if they stop us from developing and growing by keeping us stuck in the same rut and leading to destructive behaviours towards ourselves and others.

A lot of people report that they simply don't know why they react a certain way in a given situation. Indeed, they may not even be aware of how they are responding and how it affects those around them. Often the reason is a lack of understanding of the underlying emotion from which the behaviour stems. This is how bad habits are created. The emotion or impulse comes first, the behaviour second.

By observing our reactions and taking note of them we can start to explore what our emotional triggers are – the people, events and situations that create strong reactions in us. These powerful emotional responses lead to behavioural patterns or habits, so by understanding the trigger we are getting to the root of what is causing the habit and can thereby change it.

Mood diary

Make a list of all the bad habits you feel you currently have.

Start keeping a journal or make a note below on a daily basis for the duration of this section of what your moods are and how they shift during the day. Record if your emotions are fluctuating depending on what you eat and drink – especially in relation to red meat, refined sugar, lack of water, alcohol and prescription or street drugs.

Start to be observant of your body language. This will provide you with clues on how you might feel about a person or situation. Are you closing yourself off? Holding yourself back or tensing up? Covering your mouth and not speaking out? Getting a sinking feeling in the pit of your stomach? Are you lashing out, losing patience, reaching for the biscuit tin or engaging in some other deflective behaviour?

In the evening, take a few moments to reflect – retrace your steps and look at what situations you found yourself in when the mood set in. By doing this you will soon discover which situations, places and people affect you in particular ways. After a while you will start to see patterns.

Review your bad habits list and match it to your mood patterns. Try to see if there is any correlation between the people and situations you have identified as bothering you and any ensuing reactive, negative behaviour or bad habits.

Notes:

Exercises throughout this section ◇   Exercises throughout the book
Exercise and eating diary   Wake up with gratitude
Mood diary

Day 4

Choosing the habits
that you want

We first make our habits, then our habits make us.

John Dryden

We define a 'good habit' as a behavioural response that gets the desired result quicker, more effortlessly and with a positive, constructive effect on ourselves and our environment. As discussed above, by understanding our emotional triggers we are getting to the root of what may be causing the habit and we can thereby change it or choose it.

The next step from yesterday's exercise is therefore to *remember* how certain situations affect you and thus be prepared beforehand. The journal-keeping is essential in this process. Magic happens when the emotional states are no longer 'surprises' – they start to lose their power, thereby making it easier to control the ensuing behavioural reaction. Think of the old adage 'forewarned is forearmed'. For example, if you know a certain colleague always rubs you up the wrong way in meetings, and if you are mindful of that before you go in, it won't come as a surprise and you can control your response to that person.

Over time, situations and people will be easier to handle and eventually you might even be able to see something positive in a previously difficult situation. How? By experiencing the transition, you will have learnt how to neutralise a negative situation. Once you've done this in one instance you can replicate the process: analyse your emotional response, be prepared, diffuse the negative reaction, then choose a positive behavioural response. This will make you feel more empowered and less like a victim of circumstances that are seemingly beyond your control – a habit well worth developing!

Mood diary – negative and positive

Make a list of all the good habits you can think of that you would like to develop. Match them to any opposing bad habits that you currently feel you have. Review the mood patterns from Day 3 and your analysis of when the bad habits kicked in. Apply the 'forewarned is forearmed' approach and think about how you can turn the bad habit into a good one.

Start doing it, now, today – no more excuses!

Notes:

Exercises throughout this section ◇   Exercises throughout the book

Exercise and eating diary   Wake up with gratitude

Mood diary – negative and positive

Day 5

Manage your mind

Whether you think you can or whether
you think you can't, you're right!

Henry Ford

Meditation is the activity of learning how to manage the
mind so that incessant and negative thought patterns
abate. Meditation is not about sitting still and doing
nothing. It requires technique and practice but the rewards are
immeasurable. In time, regular meditation practice can begin to
permeate all areas of life and we start to feel more present, connected and peaceful – which can make acceptance, forgiveness
and personal achievement easier to master. This is what Bud-
dhists call meditation in action, or mindfulness.

Today's exercise

Meditation

Prepare the space

Choose a space in your house where you will not be disturbed
by anyone, including the phone. Ideally the space should be
clean and clutter-free. Perhaps you would like to enhance the
atmosphere with candles, incense, flowers or an inspiring picture – anything that encourages calm and connectedness in you.

The ritual of clearing the space and decorating it as you wish
provides a preparation for the practice. It calms the mind and

sets your intention, which is to focus actively on meditation. According to many Eastern philosophies (e.g. Buddhism, Feng Shui, Taoism) the energy of the space is very important and will have a direct impact on the depth of your practice.

Sitting posture

Once your space is ready, sit down in a cross-legged position, gently resting your hands on your knees. Make sure your shoulders and jaw are relaxed and your back is straight. Use a cushion under the buttocks to relieve tension in the knees and hips if necessary. Relax your face and gently close your eyes. Take a few deep breaths and become aware of your body. Put your focus on any areas of tension or aches and breathe deeply with the intention of relieving it.

Breathing

Once you have settled in more comfortably, bring your attention to your breath. Breathe in through the nose and out through the mouth (though the nose is OK too). Count to three on the in-breath and three on the out-breath. Continue for ten breaths, then relax and breathe normally for ten breaths.

Repeat the cycle four times. After that, sit quietly, breathe normally and focus on the breath. Your mind may wander off as thoughts pop into your head. Gently bring your attention back to the breath. Do not get frustrated if the mind keeps wandering – this is normal and will stop with time. As soon as you feel yourself getting tired of focusing on deep breathing, just breathe normally and observe each breath, in and out.

For the first week do this meditation as often as you like but ideally at least once a day in the morning. Try to sit for a minimum of twenty minutes. As the breathing exercise becomes more comfortable you can experiment with longer counts on the in- and out-breaths. Just make sure you don't get light-headed – this is not an endurance test! The aim is to calm the mind, lower your blood pressure and relieve tensions.

Notes:

Exercises throughout this section ◇ Exercises throughout the book
Exercise and eating diary   Wake up with gratitude
Mood diary   Meditation

Day 6

Just do it!

Genius is 1% inspiration and 99% perspiration.

Thomas Edison

For the past few days we have looked at how to develop and grow intuitively (gratitude), physically (wake up your body), emotionally (habits) and mentally (manage your mind). Carl Jung called these ideas the four basic intelligences or modes of interacting with the world. The most important thing of all is now to 'walk the walk', so today is all about just doing it! Go back and review the exercises from the last few days and make sure you are actually doing them. Reading about them will provide you with ideas and insights, but real change comes from taking action. Life is a constant spiral of opportunities, action and learning. Start twirling!

Today's exercise

Take action

Today is all about action. Try not to think too long and hard – take action instead. How does it feel to leap into something? Do you do that often and then think about what you did afterwards? Or do you tend to ponder and perhaps arrive too late to the party? Make a note in your journal of what you feel is your default mode, but for today practise not thinking too much but taking action instead; always of course with a loving and considerate intention – we are not advocating rash and thoughtless behaviour. Just have the experience of being daring.

Today's exercise: Take action

Notes:

Exercises throughout this section ◇ Exercises throughout the book
Exercise and eating diary Wake up with gratitude
Mood diary Meditation

Day 7

Build confidence, not arrogance

> To thine own self be true.
>
> **Hamlet, I, iii**

Confidence is quiet, consistent, discerning and thoughtful; arrogance is loud, erratic, non-discriminatory and selfish. Confidence does not require praise or attention; arrogance screams 'look at me'. Let's not worry about confidence – it takes care of itself. Arrogance, on the other hand, needs some work.

Arrogance is a mask for underlying insecurity. Just as before when we suggested that habits emanate from deep-seated emotions, so too does arrogance. In order to deal with it and convert it into confidence it is therefore essential to locate the insecurities that underpin it.

Self-love can be one of the hardest qualities to develop but it's an essential ingredient of confidence. Arrogance often comes from self-loathing or lack of self-respect. We love that which we look after and respect, including ourselves. The way to build true self-confidence is therefore to ask 'Do I love myself or loathe myself?'

Today's exercise

Self-love

Find a quiet moment, perhaps after your morning meditation or with your evening journal. Make a list using two columns: in the first one describe what you loathe about yourself (note: we are deliberately using a strong word here; this is about absolute honesty, not being politically correct with yourself) and in the second column, what you love about yourself.

Whatever feelings come up for you as you are doing this *allow yourself to feel them* – don't censor yourself. Cry if you want to; laugh at yourself if that feels right. This can be a very cathartic experience. Once you have uncovered what is lurking in your mind you can deal with it.

Later on in the book we will look at the act of forgiveness (Day 72) and give you exercises to be used to revisit this list and deal with the 'loathes'. For now, vow to start loving and respecting yourself. When you go to bed tonight make sure you revisit the gratitude exercise from Day 1 and include in your list all the things you love about yourself.

Today's exercise: Self-love

Notes:

Exercises throughout this section ◇   Exercises throughout the book
Exercise and eating diary   Wake up with gratitude
Mood diary   Meditation

Day 8

Stopping is not quitting, you are just taking a breath

You can live for two months without food and two weeks without water but only a few minutes without air.

Hung Yi-hsiang

As far as our physical priorities go, breathing is one most people take for granted and don't even think about. According to Daniel Reid (2003) regular, deep breathing gives an immediate boost to the circulation, parasympathetic nervous system, immune system and other vital functions; not least of all is lowering blood pressure. It is essential to breathe properly not only for survival but to ensure health and longevity.

Deep breathing comes from the diaphragm. Watch a baby or child sleeping and see how their bellies gently rise with every in-breath. That is correct diaphragmatic breathing. Most adults tend to carry tension in this area, so instead take shallower, higher breaths by raising their shoulders to their ears. During stress and emotional pressure, muscles tense up, thereby making breathing shallower still. The system thinks it is in fight-or-flight mode and releases stress hormones. The parasympathetic nervous system, which is the natural healing process, is taken out of action. Conversely, when we want to calm down, deepening our breath relaxes the system, taking us out of fight-or-flight mode.

Deep breathing practice

Lie flat on the floor with your legs comfortably bent, knees up and feet flat on the floor. Relax all tension in the shoulders, stomach, jaw and pelvis. Place one hand on your tummy and for every in-breath expand the stomach out; on every out-breath relax the stomach and let it fall back again. Repeat ten times. Relax.

Now sit up and do the same exercise. Pay attention to your shoulders so that they don't start to rise up (raising the shoulders is harder to do on the floor, but if you're sitting up bad habits can creep back in).

Once you have mastered the relaxed, diaphragmatic breathing lying and sitting, try it standing and also walking around.

Repeat this exercise over the next few days. Start monitoring how you feel emotionally after the ten deep breaths. You are hopefully feeling calmer and more focused.

Notes:

Day 9

This is your life

Your vision will become clear only when you
look into your heart. Who looks outside, dreams.
Who looks inside, awakens.

Carl Jung

Today we are putting a mirror up in front of you and asking: 'Is this what you want?' Are you living the life you want to live? If yes, are you celebrating that? If no, what are you doing about it and what are you waiting for? Do you think you are in rehearsal for your 'real' life? In that case, when does that real life actually begin? Whatever your spiritual beliefs may be, for the purposes of this discussion we are using the premise that this is the one shot you get, so what are you going to do with it?

Today's exercise

Wake up with vision

The first thing we want you to do is to remind yourself of the gratitude exercise we started on Day 1. Think about what it is you truly love; get into that loving feeling and feel really grateful to be alive. Consider how you can be more loving towards yourself and your surroundings.

Then move on to thinking about what you truly want that you do not yet have. Make sure however that none of your desires are at the expense of anyone else – there is no room for envy or jealousy in visualising your fully realised life!

Make your vision come alive: Is it seeing yourself as a more loving and generous person? How does that look? Is it owning a new house? If so, where is it, how big is it, does it have a garden, a fireplace? Is it being with a loving partner? Be clear about them – what are their qualities and attributes? Write down these dreams in your journal or below.

When the vision is strong, return to your feeling of gratitude and feel grateful that you *already have* what you just visualised, as if it had already happened.

Let these visions work their way into your daily gratitude practice. By repeating this vision daily, making it stronger and more alive, you are reaffirming your focus and intention and you are starting to make it happen. Later on in this book we will look at creating proactive and realistic goals which will serve as stepping stones to the manifestation of your vision. Action follows thought.

Notes:

Exercises throughout this section ◇   Exercises throughout the book
Exercise and eating diary   Wake up with gratitude
Mood diary   and vision
Deep breathing practice   Meditation

Day 10

Recognition and reward

The price of freedom is insecurity,
but security is often an illusion.

Lesley Garner

There is a lot of conditioning in society that tells us not to stand out from the crowd or to think we're special. Over time, this can lead to a lack of self-belief and ultimately the relinquishing of possibly the most unique aspect of being human: the ability to reflect and marvel on life in its infinite variety. But guess what? We *are* totally special. There is no one human being that is exactly the same as another. Each one of us deserves the same marvel and wonderment that all of life deserves.

Your undisputed number one fan has to be you; not in a selfish, ego-centred way but in a loving way, full of gratitude and a sense of achievement. It is wise to have a well-functioning system for self-caring, nurturing and pampering that we regularly check in with. If we wait for others to tell us that we are good or worthy we are handing over a lot of power and also losing the ability to be proactive. *We* decide when we are great. By practising loving kindness on ourselves, we also become better at being loving and kind to others.

Today's exercise

Treat yourself

Revisit your list from Day 7 on what you love about yourself. Make a new list of all the things you love to treat yourself to, large or small – anything from chocolate cake to a holiday. Reflect on where, when and how you will get these treats. Start with the small ones and go out now and do it. For the larger ones, start formulating a plan for how they can happen. Take some concrete action today such as searching online for flights or blocking off time in your diary for a break.

Today's exercise: Treat yourself

Notes:

Exercises throughout this section ◇ Exercises throughout the book
Exercise and eating diary Wake up with gratitude
Mood diary and vision
Deep breathing practice Meditation

Day 11

Stop!

The only way to get rid of a temptation is to yield to it.

Oscar Wilde

If you have followed this book from Day 1 and done the exercises on a daily basis (which of course you have!), chances are today you are feeling a little raw, a little fragile. So far, we have stirred the pot vigorously. After all, it's survival we are talking about – not of the fittest, but of you becoming the fittest you can be, the best possible version of yourself. Today is therefore about gently relaxing and letting the experiences settle. Today is a 'do nothing day'. Don't ponder too hard, don't touch your journal, eat what you want, have a lie-in, spend time with your loved ones, watch some trashy TV … You're not quitting, just taking a deep, relaxing breath.

Today's exercise

Today make time to indulge yourself and do absolutely nothing!

Day 12

Listen to your voice

It is good to have an end to journey toward; but it is the journey that matters, in the end.

Ursula K. Le Guin

How have you been getting on with your meditations? Is there still a cacophony of voices in your head when you sit down and try to concentrate? Which one should you listen to? The answer is your deeper, intuitive self, the soul voice, your heart. However you want to imagine it, it is that deeper sense of *knowing* something to be true rather than actually *hearing* it.

The way to develop this ability is to go deeper into your meditations. This is a further exploration of mindfulness which we introduced on Day 5. What you are developing is an ability to start observing yourself. Think of it as if you are standing slightly behind yourself and looking over your shoulder and thinking 'Aha! So I am meditating, and here comes a thought but I will let go of that ...' and so on. You are starting to single out that one voice you really want to hear and letting the others fade into the background.

This is quite advanced meditation practice and you might not 'catch the wave' immediately, so do not feel discouraged. We are introducing it fairly early on in the process despite its complexity as this is an invaluable tool for self-knowledge, and for many it can have a powerful impact on daily life.

Deepen your meditation

Start your meditation by focusing on your breathing. Once you have calmed your mind and feel focused on the breath imagine you are a wind gently blowing across a peaceful landscape. You gently move over mountains, rivers and forests. You see them as you pass by but you do not linger, you gently move on. The idea is that the wind represents your mind, relaxed and free, and each part of the passing landscape represents the thoughts that pop into your head.

As soon as you feel yourself getting tired or unable to retain the image in your mind, just relax and go back to your breathing. When you are ready, recall the image of the wind and landscape and muse on this image as a representation of your inner voice and the landscape as the shifting thoughts that move in and out. The wind is ever present, gently in the background, while the landscape shifts. Start feeling the difference between the two.

Conclude your meditation by saying a word of thanks for this moment of calm and connectedness and set your intention to maintain this state of peacefulness throughout your day. Whenever you feel yourself getting caught up with thoughts racing around the mind, recall the image of the wind and the landscape and go within and try to listen to that calmer, deeper voice. Take a few deep breaths as you are visualising.

Notes:

Exercises throughout this section ◇ Exercises throughout the book

Exercise and eating diary   Wake up with gratitude
Mood diary   and vision
Deep breathing practice   Deepened meditation

Day 13

Preparing for the next stage

Being defeated is often a temporary condition.
Giving up is what makes it permanent.

Marilyn vos Savant

You have completed the first of the eight stages we described in the introduction. You are at the end which is simultaneously the beginning. The start had to be about survival of the 'I'; going deep, addressing the habits and starting to eliminate the blockages that may have been there. It has been about finding a deeper, truer voice and acknowledging your needs and abilities. But you do not of course exist in isolation. Now that the 'I' has been reviewed and is on the path to deeper self-knowledge, the scope can widen. The camera is panned back. Now the 'I' has to look at the 'we', and identify the tribe. The challenge is not to lose this sense of 'I' or to get too stuck in its self-centred realm. Striking that balance is the key.

Today's exercise

I vs. we

Ponder how a balance can be struck between my individual needs and the needs of those around me. Who is dependent on me? Who do I depend on for love, work, life? How can a gentle hold of my sense of self help others to achieve balance and inspiration? How can I retain the excitement and keep celebrating myself while positively impacting others?

Today's exercise: I vs. we

Notes:

Exercises throughout this section ◇ Exercises throughout the book

Exercise and eating diary   Wake up with gratitude
Mood diary   and vision
Deep breathing practice   Deepened meditation

Tribal

Who Are My people? Do I Make a Positive Impact On Those Around Me?

Day 14

My place in the family tribe ...

Call it a clan, call it a network, call it a tribe, call it a family.
Whatever you call it, whoever you are, you need one.

Jane Howard

Who your tribe are and what your relationship is with each of them is crucial to any successful venture. Many of us find ourselves working in close quarters with people we did not necessarily choose to be with. These may be our blood relatives – those people we love dearly but sometimes find more frustrating than we can express. Or we may have the daily challenge of engaging (or not) with our work colleagues. Whatever your tribe is, you need to be able to understand their reason for being part of it, while they need to have some idea of why you are there.

At best a family can be the source of energy and passion to go out into the world and make a difference. At its worst it can cause us to question our role and function in the world. This tribal-induced anxiety can prevent us from awakening to and achieving our goals and purpose in life.

Knowing our place does not necessarily mean understanding our role in the pecking order, although this does have some value. Older members of the tribe often need to feel that their experience and years are valued and welcomed. If you are fresh to a team, especially if you are a new leader, the last thing you should do – if you want to have any hope of full engagement, support and success from your team – is disregard their past and pay no heed to their traditions, rituals and hierarchies. You may not understand, agree or give value to their past, but they do.

To understand the place where you find yourself you need to have a benchmark of feedback from those that know you or need to know you. As in all tribal traditions, the starting point of understanding who we are in relationship to who we are with is to listen to and tell stories that move, interest or celebrate.

Time with each tribe member

This is a simple yet powerful exercise which draws on the dialoguing (rather than the debating) traditions of our ancient past. Find time to sit for an hour with each member of the tribe – this could be family or work colleagues. Some of you will already be throwing up your arms in frustration at this idea: How on earth are you going to fit in an hour with each of your tribe? There are two things to bear in mind: (1) don't confuse the tribe (small, tight-knit team) with the community (those people that the tribe serve, support or collaborate with) and (2) finding a few hours early on can save days, if not weeks or months (possibly years), of life-sapping aggravation and conflict later on.

Ask them their story. What made them want to be part of this tribe? Tell them your story. Explain why you need the tribe. Seek their guidance. How can you best serve the tribe? Once you have listened and spoken then the ground has been broken and the work of planting can begin.

Notes:

Exercises throughout this section ◇	Exercises throughout the book
Time with each tribe member	Wake up with gratitude and vision
	Meditation

Day 15

What I learn from key people: Positive and negative traits

If you can't be a good example, then you'll just have to serve as a horrible warning.

Catherine Aird

There is an apocryphal story of twin brothers born in the United States in the 1950s. Their father was an abusive, alcoholic, womanising thug who spent his life involved in violent crime. He ended up on death row after being caught and convicted for a series of horrendous offences. One of the brothers followed his example into a world of criminality, addiction, drugs and all the associated demons and destruction that go with such a life. The other twin worked hard at his education, despite his lack of family support. He went on to lead a very successful life as a family man and pillar of his local community. When the brothers were asked why they had turned out as they had they both gave the same reply: 'With a father like mine, I had no choice.'

What this story highlights is that there is always a choice. While we may feel that we have no alternative, in a very real way, *we* decide if we have choice or not. It is about our perception of our power to act, rather than our inability to engage. When it comes to defining our values we are of course influenced by those close to us. As children we just accept this but as we get older we can question the opinions and ideas we have inherited. We have to challenge these ideas so that we can move forward in our lives standing on a foundation of values and understandings that are true for us and not just habitual.

The following exercise is about raising your awareness of the choices you make to a very conscious level. Much of what we say can be a quick response to the immediate stimuli of where we are and who we are with. It is this dynamic relationship between who we are, where we are and who we are with that can lead us sometimes to act first and think later.

Three-second rule

Choose a period of time (a minimum of five minutes but it could be much longer) when you know that you are going to be in conversation with other people and play a game called the 'three-second rule'. Before you respond to a question think for three seconds before replying. See how this space impacts your response. If people comment on your low-gear interaction, you could explain the exercise and they could join in (depending on how well you know them). In most cases, people will not comment other than to express their gratitude and admiration that you are such a good listener.

Today's exercise: Three-second rule

Notes:

Exercises throughout this section ◇ Exercises throughout the book
Time with each tribe member   Wake up with gratitude
and vision
Meditation

Day 16

Working with colleagues

If you befriend someone, but lack the courage to correct
them, you are, in fact, their enemy.

Japanese proverb

If you have never had a disagreement or confrontation with
a colleague in your organisation, group, school or business
then you're obviously blessed enough to be working in a
perfect palace of productivity. But perhaps it feels more like a
brooding cauldron of frustration, resentment and fear. Often
we sacrifice ideas, innovation and evolution for a quiet life. Our
sometimes overwhelming desire to be part of the tribe denies
our individual need to express and explore ideas. We are talking about striking the right balance, of course, as neither an
apologetic, compliant mouse of a person or an arrogant, self-
opinionated bully are going to be useful to the tribe.

While the intention to maintain calm and order within the
group is of great value, the danger is that you can end up with
so many elephants in the room it becomes stifling just to be
there. Sometimes someone has to point at the elephant. Here is
the challenge to the tribe: Who will be the first person to point
the finger?

The moment you highlight an inconvenient truth you begin the
inevitable emotional chain of reaction from others, which will
vary from the closed 'fight' (become defensive), 'flight' (refuse
to stay and 'listen to this rubbish'), 'freeze' (become unable to
think and speak rationally) and 'flock' (go to other members of
the tribe that are close to them and plot, bitch and seek reassurance that they are right in word and deed). The opposite end
of this spectrum is the uncorking of all the repressed feelings
that have been stored away with an outpouring of emotion that

is disproportionate to the situation. These extreme reactions, however justified, are rarely helpful.

There is no way out of the need from time to time to challenge the actions or comments of others. It does not mean that you are seeking to attack them, although this may be how they feel. As the proverb above highlights, it is only through challenging our own anxiety about what might happen in the future that we are able to take action to deal with the realities of the present.

Today's exercise

Conflict resolution

If you want to address an issue with someone, use the following steps to manage the situation:

When you say – tell them what it is that they have done, identify the behaviour.

I feel – express dispassionately how you feel without apportioning blame (i.e. not 'You *make me* feel ...').

Because – give a logical reason or example of why you feel as you do. It might be that you need to highlight or draw attention to agreements that have been broken or the impact their actions are having on others or the project you are involved in.

What can we/I/you do – give them a way out. You are not seeking to escalate a problem but to resolve a conflict.

If they challenge you, then go back to step one and start again:

When you say ... I am being over-sensitive.

I feel ... angry and frustrated.

Because ... I do not want this situation to continue as people are suffering.

What can we do ... or when would be a better time to talk?

In most cases, people respond constructively to this logical and emotionally balanced approach. If not, then your best bet is to find the person in the tribe who they will listen to and ask them for their help.

N.B. If you can only get to the first two steps of the model (When you say/I feel) and can give no rational reason (Because), then it is your issue, not theirs.

Today's exercise: Conflict resolution

Notes:

Exercises throughout this section ◇ Exercises throughout the book
Time with each tribe member   Wake up with gratitude
                                                              and vision
                                                           Meditation

Day 17

Do I have trust in others?

Techniques and technologies are important,
but trust is the issue of the decade.

Tom Peters

Management and leadership guru Tom Peters made this
statement in the nineties when the world was beginning to be swept along with technological advances
that would have seemed like science fiction only a decade
before. From momentous breakthroughs in the understanding
and application of the Internet to home computing to gigantic
leaps forward in medical science and media hype, the nineties
was the decade that marked the arrival of a new generation of
working, living and learning.

In the midst of this frenzy to be early adopters and investors in
the next big idea Tom Peters was a voice of reason. Of course,
he was up there with the best of them advocating the potential of all of this new gadgetry but he was also warning not to
forget the basic principles of any strong team. Namely, do not
let your enthusiasm for the brave new world of the future lead
you to disregard the traditions of the past that brought you to
this point. Indeed, it is only by keeping such basic human values
close to our decision-making and future plans that we can maintain our healthy growth as organisations and individuals within
those organisations. Remember the dot-com collapse?

So, as the question for today asks, do you have trust in others? We are going to consider if others have faith in you later
on in the book, but today is the day you begin to discover if you
trust other people.

Building trust

This exercise is designed for the workplace but can easily be adapted to any environment where you engage with others and want to build greater levels of trust. This is a particularly good one for parents seeking to build greater independence and trust with teenage children.

Choose one person that you live with, line manage or are collaborating with professionally or personally – anyone, in fact, that you want to show that you trust and value (you can do this for more than one person if you feel up for the challenge). Agree something that needs to be done and what their role is in achieving the goal, target or task. Clarify the desired outcomes, time scale and support (materials, costs, expertise, etc.) that they need. Agree a date and time when they are going to feed back. Let them know that you are there for them to talk to if need be, but you trust them to do what they have agreed to do. Ask them if they have any questions or concerns and then wait for them to feed back to you. Do not send them an email, constantly bring it up every time you see them or ask someone else to check up on them on your behalf.

Note your own emotional or habitual tendencies to repeat the instruction, complete their sentences, do it for them or interfere. Yes, they may make a mistake or not do it exactly like you would do but that means they are learning to manage this on their own. As long as you have agreed the parameters (what, when, how, who, etc.) and made it clear that you trust them to do it, the outcomes will be better than you had planned, simply because you trusted in the intelligence and creativity of someone else.

Today's exercise: Building trust

Notes:

Exercises throughout this section ◇ Exercises throughout the book
Time with each tribe member   Wake up with gratitude
                                              and vision
                                           Meditation

---

101 Days to Make a Change   52

Should I stay or should I go?

A fear of the unknown keeps a lot of
people from leaving bad situations.

Kathie Lee Gifford

The head teacher of a school has helped turn it around from being a failing institution to an outstanding one. She has achieved this in just a few years, despite the fact that one or two people in the school had made it clear that she was not part of the tribe, and never would be.

The school is in a small English town and a core of the staff had been educated there; they left only to go to university or teacher-training college, then returned to the area to work back at the school. Over the years this core group had made newcomers (other staff members and head teachers) feel so unwelcome that they didn't stay longer than a couple of years. Small daily exclusions from informal meetings, lunchtime chats or after-school social events made it clear to those that were not able to engage in the rituals and values of the older tribal members that they would never be part of the team.

This may sound petty but when there are eight people in a staff-room and teas and coffees are made for only seven, the pain and discomfort the excluded person feels can be huge. Imagine this and related actions occurring in some form every day. How would you feel? The impact on this head teacher has been painful. While on the outside she is determined to do the best for the children and staff – even those that interpret her actions as an attack on them (see Day 16 for more on this) – it has had a devastating impact on her physical and emotional health.

When she was describing all the things she had done to seek to engage staff in activities to support the children and school, it was obvious that she'd had to battle daily to keep the school progressing. She is mentally exhausted, physically ill, emotionally drained and spiritually lost. She has tried dialogue and debate and given clear rationale and examples of best practice. She has trusted, challenged and made sure there were no elephants in the room. However, at the time of writing, there is an outing planned for all the teaching staff which has been arranged by one of the oldest staff members of the school. No classroom assistants, administrative staff, cooks, cleaners or governors are invited. The head wasn't even informed; she found out when the caretaker told her.

Our advice to her was to leave. She has tried many people-managing techniques and has been working hard at personal change. This has worked at an 'outcomes' level but not at a fundamental, tribal, heart-based level. Sometimes, enough is enough. This is not failure – it's recognition of a painful truth that, for a whole variety of complex reasons, there are some people that just may not like you or your message and may even seek to damage you through undermining behaviour.

Today's exercise

Is it working?

This exercise focuses on working relationships rather than families. While in very extreme circumstances you may want to leave a family unit, this is a rare and radical option. However, this exercise is still very powerful in highlighting whether the dynamic balance of any group – including a family – is working.

List all the things about the team, group or community which you are a part of that are keeping you there and all the things that make you want to go. Compare the two lists and then decide if it is worth the effort to continue. If you do want to carry on, then begin the process of challenging or decluttering today. Don't wait another moment. You don't have to sort it all today

---

but you do have to begin – or start the process of managing your departure.

Sometimes our biggest challenge might be to move into a world of uncertainty. 'Better the devil you know' is often used as an excuse by the fearful to create the life they both want and end up deserving.

Today's exercise: Is it working?

Notes:

Exercises throughout this section ◇ Exercises throughout the book
Time with each tribe member   Wake up with gratitude
                                              and vision
                                            Meditation

Tribal 55

Day 19

Seeing myself through others

What we all tend to complain about most in other people are those things we don't like about ourselves.

William Wharton

It is a powerful and painful truth that when someone's actions, comments or attitude annoy and frustrate us, it is often because they are manifesting a trait that we have yet to master or manage in ourselves. This is not to say that everyone who creates a feeling of unease, discomfort or despair is without fault. They may well be all the things we say they are; their actions may be intolerable and their attitude flawed. However, just because an individual is acting like a fool does not mean to say that they are not in front of another fool when they meet us.

Two opportunities are presented to us when we encounter someone who challenges us in this way: we can discover and understand what motivates and moves this person as well as seeing what motivates and moves us. Instead of immediately taking up a position of defence we can adopt an attitude of curiosity. There is a reason why people react as they do, and much time can be saved and pain avoided if we invest a little effort and engage with that person to understand why they are behaving as they are.

Engaging in conflict should always be driven by a genuine desire to understand the other person – their needs, aspirations and expectations. However, it is a normal human response to seek also to get the other person to understand our needs, aspirations and expectations.

The effort required to not act based on emotion is part of our lifelong challenge. Children have emotional responses to people and situations and then say and do things because they are driven by their feelings first and their thinking second. A genuine adult will have the same, if not a greater, intensity of emotion and then step back from that whirlpool of righteous indignation and check out the reality of what is happening before taking appropriate action. That may well be to get angry but, more often than not, other more constructive options and actions present themselves.

Open questions

Today become aware if you are open or closed in your communication. Then choose one specific conversation, discussion or meeting that you have to attend to try this technique. Don't attempt to sustain it all day at this stage.

Whatever the focus for the meeting, when you ask questions, make them specific. Do not repeat or over-complicate and make sure that your questions are open and not closed. By that we mean no 'Did you ...?' and 'Do you ...?' questions but lots of why, how, where and when questions to invite a more considered response.

This is a simple but powerful way of highlighting whether you are leading the discussion or genuinely interested in communicating with others.

You can also add the three-second rule (see Day 15) if you want to raise your level of conversation to genuine dialogue.

Today's exercise: Open questions

Notes:

Exercises throughout this section ◇   Exercises throughout the book
    Time with each tribe member   Wake up with gratitude
                                                and vision
                                             Meditation

101 Days to Make a Change   58

Day 20

Am I a team player?

To lead the orchestra, you have to
turn your back on the crowd.

Max Lucado

Playing to the gallery and seeking to be seen and appreciated by a wider audience is a common desire in the more ambitious among us. There is nothing wrong in ambition and drive. In fact, it's an essential quality in anyone seeking to improve, learn, advance and make a difference. However, there is a time and a place, and some people can forget about the team of which they are a part when someone from outside is looking on.

If you are in a position of leadership within a team this tendency to be seen from those outside the group (the boss, the board, fellow managers, etc.) as the star is a very dangerous position to find yourself in. On the one hand you have the needs of your team and on the other you have your personal career path. Here's a thought: What if your success in the future is directly linked to your capacity to support, inform, develop and care for the people you are with at the moment? What if you are being observed by others in potential positions of power and influence? What if they are assessing your suitability for personal future success based on how well you engage with your team?

You don't have to be a leader to hold this thought. It applies to everyone in the team. Anyone who is more driven by their future potential and the impression they are making on those outside the group runs the risk of neglecting the tribe. Of course there is a balance to be struck, but it is worth checking once in a while to see if you need to turn your back on the crowd and spend some time focusing – without fear of what outsiders think – on the needs and feelings of your tribe.

Be supportive

It is painfully simple to get others to feel supported. Ask them what they are doing and how they are feeling – and allow them to speak. Building from yesterday's exercise, play 'let this person finish their sentence and then ask another question'. Seek to ask at least three open-ended questions focusing on them, their needs and their concerns. Not you – not how you feel or what you did. Give them the attention and respond to what they have said as if you are interested.

At the end of the day, write a few words in your journal or below about what you did and what the impact was on you and the person you were listening to.

Today's exercise: Be supportive

Notes:

Exercises throughout this section ◇   Exercises throughout the book
Time with each tribe member   Wake up with gratitude
                                                              and vision
                                                             Meditation

Day 21

Helping hands

He who is ashamed of asking is afraid of learning.

Danish proverb

It is an inevitable by-product of a Western educational system which focuses on competition, testing and 'getting the right answer' that many of us who have been through this factory-focused approach to child development think that we are expected to have all the answers. If we don't know the answer we need to find it out on our own – no cheating by looking at the back of the book or asking others! One of the great benefits of tribes and teams is that there are others around you who have similar values, challenges and interests. They are the people who can help, so what is holding you back from making the most of their tribal wisdom?

Ego and fear are two elements that can stupefy the most experienced and oldest among us. The perception in the tribe might be that as you are one of the 'elders' you should be able to provide definitive answers to many questions. But what happens if you don't know? What will people think of you if you actually used those words? What if you not only said you didn't know, but you needed some help? Well – and this might come as a knock to your ego – most people wouldn't care. In fact, when someone within the group comes to them for help, especially if that person is one of the older members, the person being asked for assistance will feel honoured. We don't just help ourselves when we ask others for guidance and support – we give them an opportunity for their own confidence to grow.

With such a win-win aspect, why won't we do it? Back to ego and fear again. Our little ego cannot bear the fact that we need help because we have always been 'top of the class'. Our fear is that people will think we are stupid or lacking in some way.

Remember that child in your class who was ridiculed because they weren't the brightest button in the box? Memories and emotions linger and lie. They become distorted over time and layer our present actions with future fears.

There is no shame in not having the right answer. The tragedy is in lacking the courage to ask the question.

Ask for help

Build your help muscles! Today ask for help from someone, even if you don't need it. It's good for you and good for them. Over the remaining eighty-one days, regularly make a conscious effort to ask for help. Keep a note in your journal of the impact of this on you and others.

That's it. It might sound simple but if you're someone that has always been expected to know the answers (and take pride in having this status) this could be a real challenge.

Notes:

Exercises throughout this section ◇   Exercises throughout the book

Time with each tribe member

Wake up with gratitude
and vision

Meditation

Ask for help

Day 22

Opening up the dialogue

The happiest conversation is where there is no competition, no vanity, but a calm, quiet, interchange of sentiments.

Samuel Johnson

When was the last time you sat down with your family, work colleagues or a group of good friends and had a proper conversation about things that matter to you all? It's all too easy to be like the proverbial ships that pass in the night – grabbing moments here and there to talk about practical arrangements and exchanging cursory greetings, without going too far below the surface. If this is our default position then we can begin to take each other for granted and forget to see one other as cherished members of the tribe.

We may find that we have to invest proper time to really sit down and exchange ideas, thoughts and feelings. This means that we need to timetable it into our schedule. It can feel formal and self-conscious to plan these things, especially with our families, but this could be exactly what is required if we are to stay up to speed with those that truly matter to us. The most obvious time to have a relaxed dialogue is over a meal. Sitting around the table, sharing food and time with others is a wonderful opportunity to dig deep into subjects and maybe even discover new aspects of each other.

Good dialoguing involves being able to listen as well as speak. Active listening means respecting the speaker enough to focus on what they are saying without wishing to dive in with an opinion or finish the other person's sentence. All too often we want to proffer our own viewpoint as soon as we can or we may be stuck on 'transmit', where we railroad other people's voices, forgetting that they may have equally valid perspectives. This is about having a dialogue, not a debate! We need to stay mindful of this if someone in the group has a tendency to enjoy the spotlight and the sound of their own voice.

Good dialoguing also requires a level of discipline that we may be unused to, but it gives us the chance to truly absorb and digest what other people around us are saying. It can be helpful, too, to introduce a subject or a theme. Again, this may feel forced and a little embarrassing at first but it will reap rewards in terms of feeling witnessed and understood.

Today's exercise

Good dialoguing

Make the time or plan a date in the future where you will sit and eat with your family, work colleagues or friends and have a proper conversation. Consider giving it a structure – such as each person introduces a subject (What was the most significant thing that happened to you this week? What did you find the most challenging aspect of your day?) or perhaps something more philosophical (about people's values, etc.) – around which everyone has a chance to talk while the others listen. Try to practise active listening and suggest that nobody talks at the same time as anyone else. Note how different the experience is: Was it successful? Did people feel awkward? Did you learn anything new about each other? Did it become an argument? Is it something you should do more regularly? How challenging was it to make the time?

Today's exercise: Good dialoguing

Notes:

Exercises throughout this section ◇   Exercises throughout the book
Time with each tribe member   Wake up with gratitude
and vision
Meditation
Ask for help

Tribal   65

Day 23

Valuing my people

I've learned that people will forget what you said,
people will forget what you did, but people will never
forget how you made them feel.

Maya Angelou

Following on from yesterday, today we are going to think about all the positive aspects of the groups that we identify with. Whether it's family, friends or work colleagues, what is it that binds us together? What unites us in terms of our values, ideals and history?

The people who really know us can give us strength when we need it, a trusted support mechanism and a place to truly be ourselves, where we know we are accepted and understood. The unconditional nature of this love and care provides us with a base camp from where we can go out into the world, take risks and embark on bold endeavours, knowing that we can rely on a place where we can rest and take refuge when life becomes too pressurised. These are the people that we don't have to explain ourselves to because they know who we are in our depths. If you're lucky enough to have this as a constant in your life, then it's important to acknowledge and celebrate it. Appreciating what you have means that life becomes more meaningful and you are able to invest in the right relationships without taking them too much for granted.

The people that matter

In your journal take time to acknowledge the people in your life that truly matter and keep you grounded. What is it that unites you with them? Focus on the positive events and moments that have bound you together thus far. How have they supported you and what have you done in return? What are your positive qualities as a group? How do you celebrate your togetherness? What is your shared language (humour, short-cuts, anecdotes, etc.)? What does it mean to you to have these people in your life?

Today's exercise: The people that matter

Notes:

Exercises throughout this section ◇   Exercises throughout the book
Time with each tribe member   Wake up with gratitude
and vision
Meditation
Ask for help

Day 24

Stop!

Learning how to be still, to be really still and let life happen
– that stillness becomes a radiance.

Morgan Freeman

Today is an opportunity to reflect on what you've been focusing on so far and to slow down. Don't worry about trying to achieve anything or tick anything off on a list. It's your free time and about staying in the present and enjoying whatever the day has to offer. Just take the pressure off and allow yourself to be here now!

Today's exercise

Enjoy yourself!

Day 25

Create a family event

If I want to be loved as I am, then I need to
be willing to love others as they are.

Louise Hay

How much quality time do you spend with your family? If you don't have an immediate family group that you live with, think about the family you grew up with. How often do you speak to them or see them? Perhaps you live far away and it isn't practical to see them as much as you'd like. Or you may not be a particularly close-knit unit or have active relationships with your parents or siblings, or your parents may have passed away.

Most of us have some remaining family members, even if they are great aunts or distant cousins twice removed! It's useful to remember that these relationships could have a lot to offer us in terms of people who may have known us all our lives and therefore have a unique perspective on who we are. Some of us may try to put a lot of distance between our nuclear family and who we are today. Are there relationships that could do with mending? Or old patterns or behaviour that just don't fit with who we are today? Sometimes as teenagers or adolescents people go through extended periods of rebellion or estrangement from their parents in order to become individual and distinct from the family unit. This is only natural – we need to have independence in order to discover who we are and how we differ from our tribe. Some of us may stay in that place and want to be separate, yet most of us are able to get to a point in our adult lives where we see how valuable and important our families are to us and how they have contributed to making us who we are.

Family landmarks and milestones automatically suggest themselves for parties or gatherings – birthdays, anniversaries,

Christmas and so on. Of course it's traditional to celebrate these events together, surrounded by our nearest and dearest, but why not ring the changes and think about getting your family together just for the sake of it? It could be a hearty meal, a theatre visit or even a trip away together – whatever feels appropriate. The important aspect is to remember that you only get one family and it's all too easy to take them for granted and forget where you came from and who helped to shape you.

Family reunion

Try to consider a way to bring family members together to celebrate where you are today and, if necessary, to re-establish bonds. Think about venues and dates. Weigh up who you want to invite and what would be appropriate for you all to do. If there are any negative issues around family dynamics consider how you can navigate them. Try to remember that your overriding, positive intention is to spend quality time with the people you are related to and who are, essentially, on your home team. Will this help you to become a stronger and more supportive unit? If this exercise is an impossibility, why is it? Are there realistic things you can do to address difficulties within your family?

Today's exercise: Family reunion

Notes:

Exercises throughout this section ◇   Exercises throughout the book
   Time with each tribe member   Wake up with gratitude
                                  and vision
                                  Meditation
                                  Ask for help

Day 26

Time for friends

A true friend is one who knows all about you ...
and likes you anyway.

Christi Mary Warner

How do you define friendship? And how many long-standing, solid relationships do you have with people you would class as friends? Friendships can resemble family for many people who are far away from their blood relatives or, for whatever reason, don't have much contact with them. The advantage of friendships, of course, is that they are relationships we can actively choose to invest in. We are under no obligation at the outset and usually are drawn to people with a similar worldview, sense of humour, sensibility or levels of experience in terms of background or work. Naturally friendships need extra maintenance from time to time and are certainly not to be taken for granted. Like most things, there's also a balance to be struck: perhaps the ones that need the most work or dutiful upkeep aren't necessarily the truest ones.

How many times have you temporarily lost touch with someone that you've made a strong connection with and then found you are able to pick up exactly where you left off when you meet up, whether six months or even six years on? Why does that happen? It's as if we have a profound understanding and empathy on a fundamental level and know that this bond has been soldered forever. There's a chiming of values, a deep mutual regard. This essential appreciation of the other allows us to be truly ourselves with that person; we realise that we can be natural and don't have to be on our best behaviour.

If we're lucky enough to have such cherished friendships, it's important to keep fuelling the fire and to invest time and effort in seeing people. It is also beneficial to surround ourselves with people who we know have our best interests at heart – who are therefore able to be honest and direct with us. Being known and witnessed by these people gives us a solid and dependable support network.

Fuelling friendships

Who are the friends you see the most of? Do you feel relaxed and able to be truly yourself around these people? Are these the relationships that you feel you want to invest in or do you maintain the connection through force of habit or a sense of duty? Are there people you miss talking to and being with that you don't see enough of? Think about ways to remedy this.

Today's exercise: Fuelling friendships

Notes:

Exercises throughout this section ◇   Exercises throughout the book
   Time with each tribe member   Wake up with gratitude
                                           and vision
                                           Meditation
                                          Ask for help

Section 3

Self

Who Am I?
Putting My Flags In the Sand

Day 27

Identify values

*We are what we do. Excellence then
is not an act, but a habit.*

Aristotle

A key step towards personal fulfilment and realising personal goals is understanding who we are in our depths. If we are armed with information about our aspirations and why we behave in the way we do, we can move forward with purpose, confidence and clarity. Cultures, families and work groups may share a stated set of values that create expectation, traditions, safety and a sense of worth. Our personal values are those positive aspects of ourselves that dictate the way we think and, hopefully, behave. They are our judgements about what is important in life – our individual yardsticks that determine how we see the world and the priorities we give to the things that we choose to do and the people we spend time with.

Have you ever considered what your 'non-negotiables' are? Spending valuable time identifying and focusing on your innate attitudes can be hugely informative when it comes to decision-making. It may also help you to realise what has been self-generated and what has been passed down to you through the generations.

Ultimately, your value is as good as how you treat yourself, the company you keep, the beliefs you hold and the life you lead. Are you living your values? Actively embodying your values is a hugely powerful tool that will help you to be the person you want to be. The first step however is identifying what they are. Once you have defined your own particular set of guiding principles, you can then choose knowingly to foster environments, situations and relationships where you can actively live them in freedom – they will impact on every area of your life. Then you can say you are truly being yourself and living from the best part of yourself with no division within.

Examples of positive values: compassion, equality, integrity, service, responsibility, power, respect, dedication, loyalty, honesty, innovation, accountability, dignity, love, collaboration, success, empathy, courage, wisdom, independence, security, challenge, influence, discipline/order, generosity, persistency, optimism, dependability, flexibility, sense of adventure.

Today's exercise

Live your values

Give yourself twenty minutes in a calm space with your journal. Close your eyes, take some deep breaths and connect with your depths, allowing any brain chatter to be stilled. Focus on what you acknowledge to be your values and make a list of your top ten in order of importance. Try not to rush this – allow yourself to be surprised. Think about your relationships, the positive, growthful choices you've made in the past, the actions you've taken. What inspired them? What aspirations are lurking within?

Once you have your list, now make another alongside it. This time, think about the things that you try at all costs to steer clear of in your life – the negative, frightening concepts or beliefs that can hold us back, put the brakes on our progress, make us doubt ourselves and block us from moving forwards.

> **Examples of negative values**: fear, jealousy, loneliness, failure, laziness, greed, depression, judgement, illness, impotence, rejection, disillusionment, selfishness, mean spirited, stinginess, self-importance, intrigue making, know it all, cold hearted.

Number them in order of importance (i.e. what looms the largest at this point), then compare your two lists. You may find some interesting correlations. You may have 'love' as your number one value and 'loneliness' top in the list of negatives. Now think about how much energy you've put into avoiding the negative list and how much you've put into actively living, embodying and promoting your unique list of values. You may be shocked to realise that you actually expend a lot of energy fire-fighting those negative tendencies or fears and forget to aspire to live your values.

Focus on how it's possible, on a daily basis, to move towards those positive, constructive attitudes and to let the negatives recede in importance.

Today's exercise: Live your values

Notes:

Exercises throughout this section ◇ Exercises throughout the book

Wake up with gratitude
and vision
Meditation
Ask for help

Day 28

Tests and trials: What do I call on to overcome adversity?

Opportunities to find deeper powers within ourselves come when life seems most challenging.

Joseph Campbell

Another step to knowing who we are is understanding and appreciating our capacity to triumph in the face of difficulty, however huge or humble. Sometimes we marvel at those around us who seem to navigate their way through trauma or difficulty and come out the other side relatively unscathed. If we ask them how they did it, often people respond with 'I had no choice'. As discussed earlier, they did have a choice – they just didn't see the option of giving up or caving in. They *unwittingly* chose to put their face to the wind, to keep calm and carry on, to rely on inner resources to drive them through the difficulty. We all encounter the accidents of life – we can't avoid them, and if we put energy into trying to we will undoubtedly suffer more. Change (whether internal or external) brings with it unforeseen pitfalls or variables that we may not have considered. We need to develop a constructive attitude to our fear of change – fear is after all a natural, human reaction. How do we make it a lever to action rather than a block? How can we use it to reshape who we are and connect with our values?

The Chinese word for crisis (危机) also means opportunity. Though it may not feel like it at the time, we have an opportunity to discover our own treasures within if we are forced to dig deep and draw on our inner strength when life throws us a curve ball. Often we realise this with hindsight. It's hugely valuable to reflect on those discoveries.

Overcoming difficulties

Find a calm, quiet space where you can relax and go inward for a while. In your journal, write down any occasions you can recall in the past (or present) where you've been tested through difficult circumstances. It may have been a relationship break-down, a death, being made redundant, having to move house, an argument. What's important is that you had choices to make in terms of how you dealt with the problem.

For each one, take time to think about what resources you may have called upon within to help you navigate the problem. (You may find that you sit in judgement and immediately come up with ways you could have approached it differently, more logic-ally, etc. Let those reflexive reactions go. You did the best you could at the time.) Write down what you relied on to help you through it. What was the situation? How did you approach it? How did you trust yourself to move forward? What was instinctive? From those descriptions, make a list of the quali-ties you can specifically acknowledge (e.g. tenacity, courage, self-compassion, faith).

What has emerged in you more strongly as a result of doing this exercise? Go back to your list of positive values from yesterday. Can you add more? Can you say that you've actively lived these constructive aspects of yourself? Allow yourself to feel proud and respectful of this resilience.

Today's exercise: Overcoming difficulties

Notes:

Exercises throughout this section ◇ Exercises throughout the book

Wake up with gratitude
and vision
Meditation
Ask for help

Day 29

I toast my triumphs

Increasing our self-esteem is easy. Simply do good things
and remember that you did them.

John Roger

In the same way that we tend to focus our energies on avoiding certain pitfalls or feelings rather than adopting positive
approaches, we can also be so caught up in the details or
'white noise' of our lives that we fail to see just how much
we have achieved. Worse, if we don't value our own efforts
enough, many of us find it difficult to accept or even believe
compliments or pats on the back from others for our successes.
Maybe we have our eye on the bigger prize and don't consider
the minor triumphs as important, or we keep ripping up those
goalposts and moving them further away rather than stopping
to acknowledge just how far we've come. As effortful human
beings we can be in 'do' mode as a default position and fail to
take the time to see how many small moments of success are
slowly paving the way towards our more obvious goals.

Just for today, allow yourself the opportunity to consider
your achievements over the past year. Try not to get hooked
into 'shoulds' and 'oughts' and 'if onlys'. Hindsight will always
allow us to identify ways to improve and redouble our efforts,
or see ways of doing something differently or better next time.
Instead, take the time to see how you have moved forward in
your personal and professional life. It may be a new job, a new
relationship, facing a problem head-on, passing an exam, moving house, visiting a country you've always wanted to see and
so on. They don't have to be huge moments. It can be extremely
useful for us to spend time thinking about the smaller flags in
the sand that helped us make progress. Finally, remember to
stay focused on you rather than comparing yourself to others.

Comparison is counter-productive and irrelevant when it comes to our own bespoke path.

Collage it

Take some time to identify and bask in your own successes and toast your triumphs. Looking back over the past year, clarify the moments or incidents that have helped move you to where you are now. They may not be obvious at first, but allow yourself the time and space to consider the milestones, however minor. List them and spend time acknowledging each one with pride and a sense of fulfilment. What do these achievements tell you about yourself? What aspects of your character do they illustrate?

A creative and celebratory extension of this exercise is to do an end-of-year collage. Gather together all the photographs, travel tickets, email print-outs, newspaper cuttings, certificates, cards and so on that remind you of what you did over the last year to give you a sense of achievement and to keep you moving forward. You don't have to do this at the calendar end of each year – you can start it right now, if you wish. Framing the collage so you can look at it for inspiration can be extremely satisfying and motivating.

Notes:

Exercises throughout this section ◇	Exercises throughout the book
Collage it	Wake up with gratitude and vision
	Meditation
	Ask for help

Day 30

What are my deep aspirations?

All successful people are big dreamers. They imagine what their future could be and then they work every day toward their distant vision, that goal or purpose.

Brian Tracy

'You've got to have a dream. If you don't have a dream, how you going to have a dream come true?' We can all parrot the lyrics from the musical *South Pacific* but many of us consider optimistic ideals for our future to be impractical in the real world – it's the land of fairytales, of simplistic, naive fantasy. After all, we are grown-ups now, with mortgages and families and jobs and endless responsibilities. We tell ourselves it's too late, I'm too old, I'm too institutionalised by my situation, I'm too set in my ways, I can't afford it, I'm too unfit, I'd have to move house ... you fill in the gaps. It's dispiriting how thick and fast the excuses come!

Let's stop for a moment. Have you ever considered that you project your own limitations into the world? Before this book is flung out of the window, we have to acknowledge reality. Of course our lives are jammed with very real complications, depending on our lifestyle choices. The important word there again of course is *choice*. Have you stopped telling yourself that you have a choice? Even if we are seemingly locked down by the details of our circumstances, there is always an element of free will. It might just mean we have to accept a little upheaval and change if we allow ourselves to consider different ways to do things. This may be uncomfortable in the short term but if you are investing in yourself and your future, the benefits far outweigh the immediate challenges.

Today's exercise is about thinking beyond what 'is' and projecting towards what 'could be'. It's about allowing yourself to reconnect with the aspirations you had for your life (or still have) that aren't given enough oxygen or have been consigned to the past. Our dreams for our future can be renewed and grounded in the reality of today.

Being me

Spend some time reconnecting with the hopes and ambitions you had for your life and allow yourself to remember that it's never too late to be 'the me I want to be'. Focus on aspects of yourself that would like to be expressed through those ideals. Perhaps there are unexplored desires that remain within you that need to be examined and given some air.

Take your journal and write down what you were interested in doing or being when you were younger and the sky was the limit, however unrealistic those ideas may seem now. Consider how you can take aspects of those ambitions and allow them into your current life. For example, if you wanted to be a champion sportsperson, think about why this appealed to you. Was it to do with being outside, feeling fit, active and alive, being competitive? How can you bring some of those essential elements into your life today in a way that is practical yet fulfilling? Or if you wanted to be an actor or a writer, what qualities within you did you want to explore? How can you be more creative or expressive in your life today? Just because you haven't made a career in that area doesn't mean to say there aren't ways you can nurture the potential gifts within.

You may want to look at practical ways to change your circumstances. Perhaps you feel the need to take on a new skill for work. Spend some time considering concrete ways you can make these things happen.

Today's exercise: Being me

Notes:

Day 31

The chattering monkey: Does it rule me?

Argue for your limitations, and sure enough, they're yours.

Richard Bach

As sentient beings, we are blessed with a magnificent array of cognitive functions, many of which are controlled by our organising, categorising and descriptive left brains. Our left brain helps us to make sense of the past and the present and to project into the future. It is forever analysing and calculating and is a magnificent multitasker.

While the left brain likes to identify patterns and process information, it is also capable of criticising, judging and filling in gaps for us. In other words, it is driven to try to translate the world by creating stories for us, sometimes based on a paucity of facts. This ability to tell ourselves tales can ratchet up either positively or negatively, according to how strongly we feel about a person/situation. It's that part of you that allows you to have fictitious conversations with people, so you can find yourself feeling very angry or emotional when in reality you haven't actually had a real exchange with the individual in question. It's also the part of us that can seemingly sit around a boardroom table making judgements and observations that aren't always helpful – the voices (which may be 'old tapes' playing from when we were criticised as children) that have free range to dig at us or tell us we're not good enough or clever enough. We need to learn to be gentle with these voices. If we struggle against them we are giving them too much credence.

It may be helpful to know that all of us have these voices – even the people who seem totally comfortable and secure in their own skin. The key is learning not to hook into them too much.

Acknowledge that they may have something to say but try to stay constructive and positive. Understand that they are perhaps there to protect you but also realise that they over-compensate and can be counter-productive and downright mean.

Remember that nothing worth doing gets done until we learn to deafen ourselves to some of those controlling voices. Ignore all the nay-sayers inside you and put your ideas and desires out there. Turn the tanker around in the ocean and try to say 'yes' to yourself more often.

Today's exercise

Just be

Find a quiet, peaceful space, where you feel relaxed and away from distractions. Sit or lie in a comfortable position – allow yourself twenty minutes. Close your eyes and focus on the sensation of your breath as it enters your nostrils and fills your belly. Slowly allow yourself to relax, letting go of tense muscles, breathing into any areas of tightness or unease. Allow any noises in the room or outside the window to be part of the soundscape. As the inevitable thoughts/ideas/distractions surface, acknowledge them but let them scud by like clouds. Observe any voices that want to be heard but don't get involved in dialogue with them. You're not in the market for problem-solving or answering your questions right now. Come back to your breathing each time you feel yourself carried away. Allow yourself just to be.

Today's exercise: Just be

Notes:

Day 32

Managing change

Security is mostly a superstition. It does not exist in nature. Life is either a daring adventure, or nothing. To keep our faces toward change and behave like free spirits in the presence of fate is strength undefeatable.

Helen Keller

Change is inevitable. Whether it's a sensation that develops internally (e.g. you realise with growing unease that you are no longer as happy or fulfilled in a job or relationship) or something that comes out of the blue (e.g. a death or a redundancy), it serves us well to learn to accept that nothing stays the same forever. This is particularly challenging when we feel the need to be in control of every area of our lives – those rare times when the stars seem to be in alignment, we enjoy and are fulfilled by our work, we've got a roof over our heads and are in a stable, happy relationship. When those precious ducks are all in the right row it's tempting to want to find as many ways as possible to make sure that things stay exactly as they are. You may succeed for a while but life has a funny way of throwing those aforementioned curve balls at us – and sometimes we'll be lobbed a few at a time. At such times, it can feel as if the world is testing us and that life is asking more of us than we think we can give. We may feel uncomfortable, frightened and unsure. However, life isn't so much going against us as it is encouraging us to grow.

If we struggle against new challenges we will suffer. So it's in our interests to develop a positive attitude to embracing the new, to 'keep our faces toward change and behave like free spirits in the presence of fate'. In this way we help ourselves to grow in autonomy and not leave ourselves behind, or stay in skins we've grown out of. Any initial discomfort we experience when expanding our comfort zones diminishes gradually as we begin to understand that temporary discomfort is a small price to pay for the evolution of our soul. Not only do we end up learning and growing but we inevitably become more compassionate to the challenges of others.

Today's exercise

Overcome your fears

In your journal, take some time to think about your attitude to change, now and in the past. How have you dealt with any life-changing developments? What has stopped you from accepting life's challenges or embracing new things? It's usually fear of the unknown – of being embarrassed, humiliated or unable to cope. The situations, activities and individuals that frighten us remain static. Fear, on the other hand, self-magnifies. It is when you are afraid and envisioning all that might go wrong that the energy underlying your fear grows. Today, consider the challenges you face that make you fearful. How can you address them and liberate yourself from their negativity? How can you use it to motivate you to move forward – to turn it into fuel rather than a brake or a block? When you see the heights of accomplishment you can attain when you walk through your fears, your faith in yourself will grow, allowing your next step to be easier. Make a note of the changes that you'd like to make and what attitude you'd like to foster to embrace it.

Today's exercise: Overcome your fears

Notes:

Exercises throughout this section ◇ Exercises throughout the book
Collage it Wake up with gratitude
and vision
Meditation
Ask for help

Self-sabotage:
How to avoid the traps

No one can make you feel inferior without your consent.

Eleanor Roosevelt

D o you ever find yourself in situations where your inner life doesn't match your outer one? In other words, where you are feeling a certain way inside and then act counter to those emotions? This can happen frequently in relationships – intimate, family, work or friends – when we say or do things to ensure that we will be liked, loved or respected more than we suspect we already are.

Self-sabotaging behaviour can take many forms. We may find ourselves on the brink of a longed-for success or a significant achievement and somehow feel unable to see it through, or start to feel paradoxically uncomfortable or self-critical when things are going our way. We may have a looming deadline and find ourselves doing anything but getting down to the task in hand, meaning that we ultimately give ourselves more pressure and less chance of doing a really good job. These moments give us an opportunity to examine our reactions and self-limiting beliefs to try to understand their context.

Ideas about ourselves often start in childhood, where we hard-wire a half-formed attitude about who we are through the reactions of others. We can find ourselves adding to these core beliefs and creating and recreating situations and experiences to validate them. If we have a negative self-perception, then we will at some point seek to create a moment of self-sabotage that can lead to more low self-esteem that tells us we were right to feel unworthy of happiness, success, love or security. This may sound harsh and perhaps counter-intuitive, but many of us have periods in our lives where we operate in this way at a subconscious level. If you tend to view the world through a negative lens, you are more likely to have negative self-talk and more likely to self-sabotage in order to be proved right about your negativity.

The attitude with which we approach something will have a substantial impact on the outcomes of that experience. For instance, if you go into a relationship thinking it won't work or take on a project thinking it will fail, then you may well be proved right. The good news is, once you're aware of these tendencies, you can monitor your thoughts and try some new ones on for size! Creating positive and constructive thoughts can take discipline and time but it will ultimately liberate you from limiting behaviour and giving yourself away.

Today's exercise

Create constructive thoughts

Spend some time writing down all the ideas you have about yourself that take you away from being authentic and feeling positive (e.g. I'm not clever enough to apply for that course, I'm not the sort of person who takes risks, I'm not attractive enough to be in a relationship, I can't save money, I don't deserve to be happy, I can never stick to a plan).

Choose one or two to focus on – the ones that you feel habitually get in your way and prevent you from thriving or moving forward. Alternatively, perhaps there is something currently on the radar that you want to address. Try to feel compassionate towards yourself – there's no point in feeling angry, ashamed or frustrated – try to stay on your own side. This exercise is about checking our perceptions of ourselves and being constructive.

Think of ways to reverse these attitudes. What can you replace them with? For example, 'I'm not clever enough to apply for that course' could become 'I want to do this course because ...'

Today's exercise: Create constructive thoughts

Notes:

Exercises throughout this section ◇   Exercises throughout the book
Collage it   Wake up with gratitude
and vision
Meditation
Ask for help

101 Days to Make a Change   **96**

Day 34

Fit for life?

To insure good health: eat lightly,
breathe deeply, live moderately, cultivate cheerfulness,
and maintain an interest in life.

William Londen

D o you live 'in' your body and do you have a good relationship with it? Are you aware of its needs and able to monitor its reactions? These may seem like odd questions but all too often we are guilty of taking this remarkable machine for granted. A favourite overheard quote from a very cerebral lecturer is: 'Our bodies are there to move our heads around from meeting to meeting.' Take a moment to think about how much care and respect you give to your body. Some of us need to stay in touch with our health regularly – we may have a condition such as diabetes or arthritis that requires us to stay vigilant and listen to the messages from our body. Do you only tune in when something appears to be wrong or do you take your whole self with you wherever you go?

Be reassured that you're not about to be patronised with a holier-than-thou lecture on the finer points of health, nutrition and fitness. We all know what we should be doing and how often it's a good idea to do it. For some of us, however, exercising takes on the guise of a boring chore that is always shoved to the bottom of the list and sensible eating sounds like a strict and dull regime that will only deprive us of the things we love to eat.

Of course, this is all about finding the right balance and reframing how we look at reward and indulgence. The ability to delay gratification is what separates adults from children. A blow-out, three-course meal five nights a week with little or no activity around it will ultimately make us feel sluggish and put on weight, whereas the odd rich and calorific treat and glass of wine is fine as long as we eat a variety of foods and are relatively active. It's the 80 per cent/20 per cent rule: if we eat well and healthily and keep active 80 per cent of the time, then 20 per cent of the time we can indulge ourselves.

Getting back in touch with feeling holistically fit, youthful and energised means you are better able to tackle mental challenges and daily stresses because you are in optimum health. It's not about treadmills, tape measures and salad! There are plenty of ways (if you don't already have a routine or a practice) to get back in touch with your vigour and vitality – from country walks and hot yoga to Tai Chi and frequent massage – as well as making sure we get enough sleep. Try to see this as healthy selfishness rather than something that gets in the way of other pressing activities or engagements; see discipline as something that you do *for* yourself rather than *to* yourself.

Incorporating activity and healthy eating into your life is hugely worthwhile. It ensures you have the energy to be efficient and capable at work and present for your family and friends, and it may also prolong your life. Ultimately, the combination of regular endorphin release and healthy eating can improve your mental health too.

Today's exercise

Tune into your body

Spend some time tuning into your body and interpreting what it needs. Find a quiet, comfortable place where you can relax, preferably lying down. Make sure that you are warm and cosy as you will be lying down for about twenty minutes. Lie in a semi-supine position (i.e. with your knees raised and feet flat on the floor – you may wish to place a book or a pillow under your head so that your neck is free and lengthened). Focus on your breathing and allow your body to dissolve into the floor. As your mind wanders, make sure you don't get caught up in

---

any concerns or issues; keep coming back to your breathing to ground you. Think of your spine as the anchor point, with the floor coming up underneath to support you. Your muscles and tissues are falling away from your spine and melting into the ground. Enjoy the sensation of support and relaxation. As you breathe more deeply, imagine you are breathing in a pure, cleansing turquoise light. Mentally scan your body, from the top of your head to the tips of your toes, searching out any tense, aching or painful areas. Direct your breath into those places. Enjoy the sensation. Imagine your veins are full of sparkling, fizzy liquid. Track the sensation of it flowing around your body. Keep coming back to your breathing, enjoying the sensation of well-being as it floods your body.

After twenty minutes, roll onto one side, into the foetal position, then slowly get to your knees and roll slowly up your spine, with your head coming up last. Hold on to the feeling of being refreshed, and take some time to consider how you can introduce more activity into your life. Maybe it's about walking a neighbour's dog, walking to the station rather than getting a bus or a cab, playing badminton or even taking the time to do some simple stretches every day.

Notes:

Exercises throughout this section ◇ Exercises throughout the book
Collage it

Wake up with gratitude
and vision
Meditation
Ask for help
Tune into your body

Day 35

Three questions for me

*Anyone can get old, but growth only comes
with effort and commitment.*

Phillip Humbert

Just as a car needs a regular MOT, so it makes sense for us to carry out a general review of our progress at particular times in our lives. We've already mentioned how wise it is to be ready to adapt to the vagaries of change; this process is one of the ways we can keep ourselves on our toes and match fit to meet the challenges of our lives.

Time invested in focusing on our unique qualities and attributes, as well as those areas we may need to dedicate effort to grow, means that we don't waste precious energy trying to be things we're not. If we can acknowledge who we are and work with that rather than trying to emulate or adopt other's blueprints of behaviour means we are serving ourselves in a hugely constructive way. Remember: comparison is deadly! Work with who you are and what you've got. That way you will stay true to your particular path of progress.

Today's exercise

SWIFT

The SWIFT model is a clear and common-sense way to audit your current status. It requires honesty, clarity and discipline, but if you follow it wisely it will signpost the next part of your journey and allow you to move forward with integrity, always keeping reality as your guide.

SWIFT stands for Strengths, Weaknesses, (areas for) Improvement, Focus and Task (or goal). We will look at the Focus and the Task elements later on in the book (see Days 42 and 43). For today, in your journal ask yourself three questions: What are my strengths? What are my weaknesses? What, then, are my areas for improvement?

Try to clear your mind and let go of any chatter or judgements. Sometimes we find it easier to come up with negative statements about ourselves, so try with the strengths question to focus on what you intuitively know to be right about yourself when it comes to your natural abilities. You may automatically discount something because you assume everyone is able to do it or is good at it. Make sure you stop and check in with your depths – are you in line with reality?

When it comes to weaknesses, focus on the aspects of yourself where you have challenges – skills that could be developed or negative traits that you struggle with. Again, try to resist criticising yourself; everyone has weaknesses and it takes humility to acknowledge them, but you don't have to stick the knife in while you do it. Just state them clearly and honestly.

The third question on areas for improvement is where you need to be rigorous and constructive. We are not yet looking at specific goal-setting – that comes later. Rather, move on from weaknesses and try to establish which areas in your life could do with being updated or worked on, as opposed to what negative traits you can eradicate.

Today's exercise: SWIFT

Notes:

Three questions for others

In giving advice seek to help, not to please, your friend.

Solon

Our friends, family and colleagues are a great mirror for us. We learn so much about ourselves from our relationships, and the people we choose to spend the majority of our time with know more about us sometimes than we imagine they do. They are on the receiving end of our actions and reactions and are therefore well placed to give us feedback and shine a different light on who we are.

Yesterday we looked at the S, W and I of SWIFT and you asked yourself three questions about your strengths, weaknesses and possible areas for improvement. Today you are going to ask the same questions about yourself to two others – friends, family or someone that you work with – to see what answers they come up with. It is important to see if what we believe about ourselves is the way other people perceive us. Try to choose two people from different areas of your life so that you get a spectrum, then the results will be more informative. Remember to select people who you spend time with regularly; a family member who you rarely see may mean that their focus is on past impressions that might not be current with who you are today.

Today's exercise

Just listen

Choose two people who know you well in (preferably) different contexts. Ask them 'What are my strengths?' and 'What are my weaknesses?' and what they consider to be your areas for improvement. Listen carefully and write down what they say. Try not to enter into conversation with them about their responses and don't agree/justify/complain/describe. Be aware that you will get far more from this exercise if you stay receptive and open to what you hear – you are giving yourself a gift to help you move forward.

Once you've spoken with both people, spend some time evaluating what they said and also reviewing your own answers. Are there any patterns or recurring themes? What do you instinctively know to be true, even if it is uncomfortable? Resolve to have humility before the truth and try to use this information to signpost your next steps.

Today's exercise: Just listen

Notes:

Day 37

Time for me, in nature

What is this life if, full of care,
We have no time to stand and stare.
No time to stand beneath the boughs
And stare as long as sheep or cows.

'Leisure', William Henry Davies

Getting away from the urban sprawl or a built-up environment and putting yourself in a natural context – whether it's the seaside, a wood, a hillside or a park – can be incredibly restorative. Being outside in the elements has a wonderful way of getting us out of our heads and into a new space, with a different sense of perspective and appreciation for what is. If we forget how to 'stand and stare' we run the risk of getting too caught up in the lists, logic and details of everyday life. If we are going through a particularly trying or traumatic time, being outside and filling our lungs with fresh air can give us precious moments to be comforted by the bigger picture. It may not change the details of our difficulties but it gives it a different backdrop for a while.

Today's exercise

Appreciate the elements

Today is about finding a space outside and just being in it. You may not be lucky enough to live near a river or an expanse of rolling hills but there's bound to be a park nearby or a square with some sort of greenery. Find a quiet spot and take half an hour to focus, to feel, to breathe. You may wish to sit or take a walk. Borrow a dog if you want a country ramble! Lift your gaze up – it's amazing what we fail to see above our eyeline. Look at the colours and the subtle differences in their hues and shades. Enjoy the breeze/sunshine/rain. Whatever your version of the transcendent is, you can experience it through the elements. Be grateful for your life and the life you see around you in the comforting cycles of nature and the seasons.

Today's exercise: Appreciate the elements

Notes:

Exercises throughout this section ◇   Exercises throughout the book

Collage it   Wake up with gratitude
and vision

Meditation

Ask for help

Tune into your body

Day 38

De-clutter! Prepare for action

Clutter is the end result of procrastination.

Jeff Campbell

The state of our surroundings often reflects our inner world. If you are trying to work from home in the midst of ever-growing piles of papers, books, bills, letters and coffee cups then it's pretty likely you aren't going to feel inspired or motivated to focus on the job in hand. Maybe your desk at work is so cluttered that you can't find the piece of paper you need which will set you off on today's task. We end up wasting time and feeling more stressed and frustrated when we literally can't see the way ahead.

What about your living space? Are there cupboards or whole areas you use as mini dumping grounds? Perhaps a spare room has slowly become the storage space for items that don't seem to fit anywhere else. It can be all too easy to fall into dysfunction and keep on piling up the clutter, always telling ourselves we'll get cracking on it tomorrow or next week. Sound familiar? As ever, the first step isn't to blame yourself. Start positively and get in touch with your motivation!

The feeling of liberation after a spot of de-cluttering can be surprisingly reinvigorating and will inspire you to keep going. You may even come across items that you've been trying to track down for ages. You may find yourself wondering why you've put this off for so long.

De-clutter

Start small and choose one area in your environment to de-clutter and see how you progress. Be systematic and use labelled boxes, then see if you can take some stuff to a charity shop and recycle others. If you decide you want to keep items, be clear about how much you need them. Are you hanging on to them for a reason? Is it sentimentality? Is it something that is useful for you today? Or is it perhaps a welcome source of inspiration? If it's an item of clothing, have you worn it in the past year? Do you really need to file all your birthday cards? Can you put stray photographs into one album?

Today's exercise: De-clutter

Notes:

Exercises throughout this section ◇	Exercises throughout the book
Collage it	Wake up with gratitude and vision
	Meditation
	Ask for help
	Tune into your body

Day 39

Journal

So many things bubble up inside me ... that's why I always come back to my diary. That is where I start and finish.

Anne Frank

In her book *The Artist's Way*, Julia Cameron recommends an activity called 'morning pages'. This is a disciplined, grounding ritual that ultimately keeps you in touch with the treasures that lurk within. It involves writing three pages every morning as soon as you are compos mentis, without worrying about style or finesse, without censoring your words or having a theme – in other words, it's continuous mental flossing on anything that happens to feel relevant at the time. You may want to grumble, philosophise, recount a dream, describe a relationship difficulty, express pride in an achievement – whatever feels important at the time. The content isn't the focus – the important aspect is being disciplined enough to do it every day.

Whether or not we choose to do this daily, journaling can be a hugely valuable part of personal growth. We can start to see themes or patterns; areas that require our attention can emerge and we may also end up answering some of our own dilemmas and generating new ideas and goals. If we feel blocked or at a crossroads we may begin to see which direction we need to go in. The key is patience and commitment.

Write it down

Take twenty minutes to write down whatever needs to be expressed. Make sure you can be undisturbed and take some time to focus on how you are today before you write. Choose not to plan or monitor your words – write continuously for twenty minutes without rereading what you've already written.

Today's exercise: Write it down

Notes:

Exercises throughout this section ◇   Exercises throughout the book

Collage it

Wake up with gratitude
and vision

Meditation

Ask for help

Tune into your body

Section 4

Order

Leading My Life with Solid Foundations

Day 40

Daring to dream

The greatest glory in living lies not in never falling,
but in rising every time we fall.

Nelson Mandela

In Day 9 we asked you to start visualising your ideal life. The challenge is to allow yourself to dream and at the same time be realistic about how and when to make change happen; that is, to make a connection between that which exists only in thought form and actual concrete action. Action follows thought and the greatest obstacle to fulfilment is our perception of our limitations.

What is a dream? Definitions vary from 'goal', 'illusion' or 'vision' to 'conjure up a scenario'. The implication is that our thoughts shape the dream before it can happen. We have to actively create or conjure up the scenario that we want, and then take concrete steps to make the dream come true. Breaking down the process in this way makes it a lot more achievable and less intimidating. Dreaming and creating our ideal life becomes another part of our routine that we have to plan and act on, just like our working lives, family commitments and leisure pursuits. It is no longer a nebulous concept. The difference is that we are now doing it deliberately; setting aside time and effort instead of just letting life take us in whatever direction it goes.

Revise your dreams

Revisit your dream visualisation from Day 9. Firstly ask yourself honestly if those really are your dreams. A common experience when doing this exercise for the first time is that superficial ideas of what you think you desire come to the surface because of ideals stemming from conditioning rather than what you want deep down. Be honest with yourself. Now take each dream in turn and look at your current lifestyle. Ask yourself the following questions:

- Have you moved any closer to your ideal since Day 9?

- Does your current lifestyle support your ideal or are there large discrepancies?

- What small changes can you make today to move your current lifestyle closer to your ideal?

Work your revised dreams into your daily gratitude exercise and practise feeling grateful for all the gifts you have already received.

Today's exercise: Revise your dreams

Notes:

Exercises throughout this section   ◇   Exercises throughout the book
Wake up with gratitude
and vision
Meditation
Ask for help
Tune into your body

Day 41

Review SWIFT

He who knows others is wise.
He who knows himself is enlightened.

Lao Tzu

As we've already discussed, having an informed sense of self means that we are more likely to behave with purpose and clarity and make decisions based on our true reality. On Days 35 and 36 we looked at the SWIFT model, where you sat with a family member and a colleague/friend and asked them to talk about your strengths, weaknesses and areas for improvement. This may have been a painful exercise for some of you. It can be challenging and confronting to get honest feedback from those around us, but if we trust them and appreciate that they know us best then we can benefit hugely from what they are prepared to tell us. We all need to keep journeying along our own personal path to self-improvement so this unique opportunity should be grasped with both hands – especially if their answers ring true with our own instincts.

Were you able to sit and listen to the answers they gave with humility? Or were you tempted to engage in a conversation – to justify, to disagree, to concur? This can be a natural reaction when someone tells us what our weaknesses are – it can be easier for us to identify with negative aspects more than positive ones.

Build on your strengths

Go back to the answers you were given: What were the common themes? What are the positive aspects of yourself that you can build on? Do you feel more confident because they have been highlighted and witnessed by people you trust? How about your weaknesses? Where can you put your energies in terms of addressing these? For example, it may be a matter of speaking up more, staying true to your word, having more faith in your abilities or finishing what you start. Whatever you discover about yourself which may be deemed 'negative', try to put your energies into the areas for improvement. What are those areas? Which is the one that rings most true with you, or is most helpful to focus on, given your current circumstances? This will prepare you for the next part of the exercise – the focus.

Today's exercise: Build on your strengths

Notes:

Exercises throughout this section ◇ Exercises throughout the book
Wake up with gratitude
and vision
Meditation
Ask for help
Tune into your body

Day 42

Focus: Key areas

I never hit a shot, not even in practice, without having a very sharp in-focus picture of it in my head.

Jack Nicklaus

After the discussions and feedback you have had with friends and family, what should you now focus on? After all, life is full of endless distractions, not only in the moment with phones, emails, meetings and so on, but also with worries about how life will turn out in the long run for ourselves and our loved ones. No wonder it can be hard to focus and more so knowing what to focus on.

Societal pressures often lead to an emphasis on the things that give immediate value and prestige: money, property, professional success, external beauty. The quick and easy choice is therefore to concentrate on these aspects. But great success in these areas rarely leads to a deeper sense of satisfaction, and after years of working hard, people may choose to leave their partners, they may get burnt out or have a mid-life crisis. For some, disastrously, they lose all sense of value in their lives. The misconception is that superficial achievements give satisfaction for a while, so if we simply change to another superficial achievement we will regain that sense of contentment. This kind of thinking does not address the reality that we take our issues with us into each new situation if we do not decide to look deeper and address them. It is therefore essential to shift the focus away from the trivial to our deep-seated human needs and investigate what it is that will make us truly happy.

Moving on

Think back on a time in your life when you lost focus and made a bad decision – how detrimental was that to your progress? Investigate how you perhaps missed reviewing your issues and ended up taking them with you into another similar situation. Ponder now if there is an area of your life where you are dissatisfied and you are considering making a change. Analyse if any of the same issues are present in this current situation. Ask yourself what you need to do to address those and how you can make a better decision this time. Bearing this in mind, and following the SWIFT model, decide where you are going to focus your energies in the light of the conversations you've had about your strengths, weaknesses and areas for improvement. What needs your attention? Think both professionally and personally.

Today's exercise: Moving on

Notes:

Exercises throughout this section ◇   Exercises throughout the book

Wake up with gratitude
and vision

Meditation

Ask for help

Tune into your body

Day 43

Task: Professional goals

Nothing is particularly hard if you divide it into small jobs.

Henry Ford

Now that you have identified the areas you want to improve professionally or personally, it's time to state the task or goal. Goals need to be concrete and achievable, so today we are turning the dreams and focus areas into goals. The exercise of going through the following steps will help you with a number of things: it will make a dream into an achievable concrete reality; it will help you to clarify to yourself exactly what it is you want to achieve and how hard you are willing to work for it; it will help you to let go of old ideas that no longer feel relevant; and it will provide you with a structure of how to go about proactively changing your life.

Today's exercise

Review your professional goals

In your journal write down all your professional goals. Compare them to each other one by one and determine which one has immediate priority. Take each goal or task in turn and break it down using the following structure:

- State the task or goal in the present tense and in a positive way making this an affirmation.

- Write down by when you will achieve this goal.

- Clearly state the benchmark you will use to measure that you have achieved this goal.

- Analyse what/who/how/where/when/why you will need in order to achieve it.

- Pin-point potential obstacles.

- Describe how you will reward yourself once the goal is achieved.

- Create a timeline between now and when your goal is to be achieved, stating in clear terms what needs to be done by when. This can be as detailed as you like depending on the particular goal.

- Pledge to review your goals on a daily basis to ensure you are on track and to strengthen your positive affirmations.

Be prepared to alter your goals as you go along. Sometimes you will achieve something way ahead of time and at other times, as you proceed, a certain goal may lose its value. That is all part of life and of the process of change and personal growth.

Notes:

Exercises throughout this section ◇   Exercises throughout the book
Wake up with gratitude
and vision
Meditation
Ask for help
Tune into your body
Review your goals

Day 44

Task: Personal goals

Those who cannot change their
minds cannot change anything.

George Bernard Shaw

For certain goals, notably spiritual and emotional ones, it can be harder to put a structure on our process. How do we, for example, measure when we are a more loving and attentive partner or a better friend? By going through the process of writing down even more abstract and esoteric tasks or goals, and by investigating what we might need to do to achieve these goals, we are helping ourselves make them more attainable and real. The process of repeating the goals on a daily basis also acts as a positive affirmation and will help us to make better progress.

Today's exercise

Review your personal goals

Take out your journal and write down your personal tasks and goals. Compare them to each other one by one and determine which one has immediate priority. Take each goal in turn and break it down, using the eight-step structure we introduced yesterday.

Today's exercise: Review your personal goals

Notes:

Exercises throughout this section ◇ Exercises throughout the book
Wake up with gratitude
and vision
Meditation
Ask for help
Tune into your body
Review your goals

Day 45

Time management

I find that the harder I work, the more luck I seem to have.

Thomas Jefferson

Time: friend or foe? Neither: time just is. We all have exactly the same amount of minutes available to us in a day. It's up to us how to use them. As with our focus, it is about quality not quantity. Time management is not about writing endless lists that just serve to give us a guilty conscience if we do not complete them by the end of the day. It is about knowing what our focus areas are, what our tasks and goals are, what our dreams are and making sure we spend our time wisely working towards these objectives. It is about realising that this moment, right here, right now, is actually the only time we have, so are we present, focused and ready or are we absent-minded, distracted and unprepared? When opportunity comes knocking which one of the above mindsets will enable us to capitalise on that opportunity?

Today's exercise

Time diary

Over the course of a week, keep a time diary. Write down at the end of each day approximately how much time you have spent on what activities. It is likely to both shock and amaze you what you spend your time on. Think long and hard if any of those activities need to be increased or decreased. Work the result into your goal-setting activity.

Notes:

Day 46

Systems and strategies

Vision without action is merely a dream.
Action without vision just passes the time.
Vision with action can change the world.

Joel A. Barker

These ten days are all about order and structure – a chance to review if the systems and strategies currently in operation are supporting a healthy and well-functioning life. Our systems are any of the operational aspects that help us to do what we have to do in a practical sense: transportation from A to B (work, school, etc.), health, work, living situation, financial circumstances and so on. Strategies tie in with this and identify whether any potential changes are needed in these systems in order to achieve our goals and dreams. It will give us an indication of our energy resource management. Are we continually running around chasing our tail in order to make ends meet and serve financial obligations? Do our systems allow for some downtime to think and just be – enjoying nature, a hobby or time with friends? Does our financial planning allow for a buffer against leaner times?

Today's exercise

Systems analysis

Think about your life from a 'scientific' point of view. Analyse your systems and look for energy leaks or inefficiencies. Alternatively, use the idea of seeing your life as an organisation – a school, business, family unit or charity. Are all the 'departments' working towards the same vision? Are you building for the future or heading towards chaos? How well is your resource management plan functioning? Your financial planning? Your operational planning? Are you using the right suppliers and subcontractors? Who would you fire or hire? Are all members of the organisation well nurtured and supported?

Today's exercise: Systems analysis

Notes:

Exercises throughout this section ◇   Exercises throughout the book
Time diary

Wake up with gratitude
and vision
Meditation
Ask for help
Tune into your body
Review your goals

Day 47

Support network

Integrate what you believe in every single
area of your life. Take your heart to work and ask
the most and best of everybody else, too.

Meryl Streep

In Section 2 on tribes we discussed the value and importance
of healthy relationships with family and friends. Building a
strong support network around us basically means that for
all our needs and possible eventualities we know who we can
turn to. Key to this is understanding what kind of support we
need and what we can expect of people. Not everyone is capable
of lending the same kind of help. Equally important is asking
ourselves how supportive we are towards others. The more
we invest in a relationship, the more we get out of it. Behaving lovingly and supportively are the starting points to healthy
relationships.

Today's exercise

Be actively more supportive

In your journal make a list of the people you consider to be in
your support network. List next to them what kind of support
you expect from them. Ask yourself if these expectations are
reasonable. Make another column next to the names and write
down the support functions you feel you give to them. Do you
expect the same of yourself as you do of them? If not, why not?

Make another list and write down all the areas where you feel
unsupported. Go back and review your list and ask yourself

firstly who you provide that level of support to and secondly who you could ask for that kind of help. If you feel you are missing something then start supplying others with that type of support. Over time you will start to receive the same in return, perhaps not from the same person but from someone else – maybe from an unexpected source.

Notes:

Exercises throughout this section ◇   Exercises throughout the book

Time diary   Wake up with gratitude
and vision
Meditation
Ask for help
Tune into your body
Review your goals
Be actively more supportive

Day 48

Structure: Laying the tracks

Truthfully, we don't have the faintest idea what to do.
Yet this is not an admission of defeat,
it is an invitation to experiment.

Margaret Wheatley

It is easy to want to have all the answers – to know exactly what to do next, who to involve, when it should happen and so on. The danger is that if the focus is solely on the external structures or solutions we can miss seeing when these structures no longer serve us; there is a vested interest in this situation, opinion or relationship which can cloud underlying issues. So when we talk about 'laying the tracks' we are referring to a gentle ability to question our choices on a continuous basis to make sure they still serve us. Why not toy with the idea that we don't have all the answers, and do not need to, but we do have the ability to keep experimenting because we allow ourselves to do so? By building up our experience bank of questioning and re-evaluating we become more confident in our ability to experiment and discover clever new solutions.

Today's exercise

Question your certainty

Ponder how deep the need is in you to have certainty, to know all the answers. Think about how you could view life differently if you had confidence in your ability to experiment and come up with new solutions all the time. This way it becomes less about the answers and more about asking the right questions. What new structures would that need? Would a diary for recording your personal developments help? Or having trusted friends you could check in with regularly? Or joining a meditation course to help you stay open to possibility? What do you need for your inner structures to be solid and supporting of your outer needs?

Today's exercise: Question your certainty

Notes:

Exercises throughout this section ◇ Exercises throughout the book
Time diary
Wake up with gratitude
and vision
Meditation
Ask for help
Tune into your body
Review your goals
Be actively more supportive

Day 49

Personal pledge

Live to the point of tears.

Albert Camus

The amount of time we spend on inconsequential things, such as watching television or going on social networking sites, is quite extraordinary. By the time we reach later life we may find that years could literally have been spent on the sofa – consider that! We might think there is nothing wrong with relaxing in front of the telly but let's unpick why we might need to unwind in the first place. What was it that wound us up so much that we need to be switched off to deal with it? How about if we didn't get so tense and stressed in the first place so that we wouldn't need unwinding? How about a more balanced approach to life and work so that downtime is spent more fruitfully?

Today's exercise

No-screen policy

Abandon all screens during the evening for the remainder of this week – no TV, no computer, no games. Get creative about how to fill your leisure time. Spend time out at a cultural or sporting event. Meet friends for dinner. Read a book. Do something creative. Meditate. Do nothing.

Notes:

Day 50

Stop!

'Making it' in whatever field is only meaningful as
long as there are thousands or millions of others who don't
make it, so you need other human beings to 'fail' so that
your life can have meaning.

Eckhart Tolle

Let's talk about ambition. A desire to do good, to make the most of your gifts or to provide a great lifestyle for yourself and your family can be considered worthy pursuits. What about when that spills over into greed and ego-centredness and the priority is no longer deeper satisfaction but rather the more superficial hunt for prestige and power? Is there a part of you that considers itself 'worthy' of rewards and recognition? More worthy than somebody else? Have you ever experienced that the more you get, the more you want? Where are you going to get it? What about if what you have is perfect and good enough? The journey and self-discovery it takes to realise your own talents are themselves deeply rewarding.

Today's exercise

The price of success

Think about your ambitions and ask honestly if you wish your own success at the expense of others. This can be very subtle. On the surface most of us would immediately reject this thought and say, 'But I'm a good person; of course I don't wish failure upon anyone else.' However, jealousy and envy are common human emotions. Don't beat yourself up for having them. Accept it if you do and stop wishing your own success at the expense of someone else. Celebrate if you don't. There is plenty of milk and honey out there for everyone.

Today's exercise: The price of success

Notes:

Exercises throughout this section ◇   Exercises throughout the book
Time diary   Wake up with gratitude
No-screen policy   and vision
                                    Meditation
                                    Ask for help
                                 Tune into your body
                                  Review your goals
                              Be actively more supportive

101 Days to Make a Change   138

Day 51

Doing a 360°

*A man should never be ashamed to own that
he is wrong, which is but saying in other words that he
is wiser today than he was yesterday.*

Alexander Pope

When was the last time you realised and admitted that you had got something completely wrong? Or that you wanted to change your mind about something? The truth is that new information is coming at us all the time – facts, figures, ideas, events, experiences and so on that we had no clue about sometimes just moments before. Yet there can be an unattainable desire to be in control, to feel like the right decision was made and therefore can't possibly be questioned. The problem with this is that it makes for a closed mindset instead of one which is constantly ready for and able to process all this new material.

We do not need to hold *all* of the answers, to be right *all* of the time or make life-long decisions every day; what we do need is the ability to be receptive to the ever-changing landscape life provides us with and the courage to change our minds when old decisions no longer measure up. If they do, so much the better. However, by revisiting and being open to the possibility that our opinions are not necessarily right means that we can feel even more confident that they really are correct now since they have been informed by more up-to-date information. In other words, by questioning our decisions we test them to ensure they really are accurate. We are creating a positive circle.

Check out old decisions

Think about the questions posed above about when you last admitted you had got something wrong or wanted to change your mind about something. When was the last time this happened? How did you react? Did you entrench yourself in your belief that the old decision was right? Or did you open yourself up to the need to question the idea? Ask yourself honestly if you are having second thoughts about something – review all the possible consequences if you both change or don't change your mind. What is the worst-case scenario? What is the best-case scenario? How do your personal goals compare with these scenarios? Do your goals need to be revised?

Today's exercise: Check out old decisions

Notes:

Day 52

Prepare for lift-off!

I want to know the mind of God, the rest are details.

Albert Einstein

Today you are exactly halfway through *101 Days to Make a Change*. A milestone! You have examined yourself, your relationships, your support structures, your environment and put it all under the microscope. Hopefully you have found stimulating challenges and reasons to celebrate. Some of it may have been difficult to accept, other things may have felt surprisingly easy. The key is to realise that the minute analysis and tinkering is putting your system in better shape for any upcoming challenges and allowing you to keep panning the camera back and see an increasingly complex and wondrous picture: your life.

Today's exercise

Great inspiration

Seek out the truly great, the shoulders on which you would like to stand and view the world. Is it an artist, scientist, humanitarian, freedom fighter or someone closer to home, a relative or friend? What is it about this person that makes them great? What is it that lifts them higher above the rest? Let yourself be inspired to think big – think like them, see the world the way they do. Realise that you too can rise above and reach new heights. Today you are halfway through the 101-day process, so look back and journal your experience so far. How can 'the greats' inspire you further and help you with your next chapters?

Today's exercise: Great inspiration

Notes:

Section 5

Enterprise

Moving Forward with Self-Knowledge

Day 53

Imagining success: Adopting a positive vision

Change your mind, prove you've got one, that's what I say.

Jools Holland

All thoughts are habits that have been acquired due to the interactions and experiences we have had over the course of our lives. If we've had particularly negative experiences then these can wire up our brain and psyche to be fearful or overly cautious of trying new things or believing that we are incapable of possessing certain gifts or capabilities.

During Section 5 on Enterprise we want to show you how replacing a negative vision with a more positive alternative can release extraordinary benefits in our thinking, relationships, confidence and general well-being.

The basis for this powerful release of potential is rooted in hard facts as well as abstract creativity. When the brain fires itself up with a new thought these synaptic sparks create a short-term link between the brain cells. An initial thought literally wires up the synapses in the brain and they create a connection through the transfer of chemicals. This connection is made into a pathway when myelin, a kind of insulation tape for the neural pathways, is added. Myelin is essential to healthy brain growth and is produced through repetition in thought, word and deed. Repetition of that initial idea, action or knowledge will create strong links between the synapses and be 'soldered in'. St Thomas Aquinas said we embed our learning when we 'repeat with frequent meditation'. These repetitions strengthen links and become neural pathways.

Word and deed are hard to change and thought is even harder. But, as we are going to discover over the next few days, it is possible.

Linking the present to the future

Over the past weeks you will have reflected, refocused and engaged with others in order to come up with one or two goals. Let's refine the target. If you have a goal (or goals) for the end of the 101 days (hopefully by now you do) reflect on one characteristic that would assist you in attaining this goal. It could be courage, determination, passion or something else. Take a moment to jot down one or two attributes that will support you. Now choose one.

Using one of the earlier relaxation techniques, slow down your thinking and visualise yourself manifesting this talent. Imagine how you would approach specific situations. How would people respond to you? For the next ten days, at the beginning and end of each day, repeat this positive visualisation. If and when you have a voice come into your head saying 'this is not you' or 'you are being foolish' or some other lie, recognise it as an old habit and ignore it. To assist you, we will share another technique with you tomorrow.

Notes:

Day 54

Redefining comfort

*Too often we ... enjoy the comfort of opinion
without the discomfort of thought.*

John F. Kennedy

We hope that you have begun yesterday's uncomfortable challenge of rethinking thoughts you may have about who you are and what you can achieve. It is important to remember that whatever you do, if you are seeking to evolve there will always be discomfort. There is a necessity for friction and dissonance in all creative acts.

It is the human condition to seek comfort and security. This is a central drive for our sense of safety. However, when we become comfortable in any area of our lives – be that work, relationships or other challenges we feel we have mastered – we run the risk of stagnating because we don't want the inevitable disruption to the order we have worked so hard to create.

This order is an illusion. If there were not the risk of external influences (other people or a changing world) then it might be possible to attain order and then stop the constant effort of managing change. But life is not like that. The world does not rest and is always shifting. If we are to be truly part of this dance then we have to get away from the table where we have spent so long sitting and start moving. To do any less is to be at the party but miss joining in the fun.

Pop on your metaphorical dance shoes – today we're going to take yesterday's exercise a little further.

Future focus

Put yourself in a relaxed state and focus on visualising yourself in the future, with your new or more defined positive attribute. When a negative voice comes into your head, try to grab it. Imagine it is a snake and you have gripped it strongly by the throat. It is still speaking disheartening words of doubt. Listen. Who has said this to you in the past? Who was it that planted this idea that you were not worthy? It could be another person or an earlier, more anxious and frightened you. Listen clearly to this voice that is saying you can't.

Focus on the voice and turn up the volume in your head. Make the voice very strong and clear. Now turn it down to barely a whisper and replace it with your own audio/visual positive vision. How does this feel? Now turn the positive voice down and allow the negative to come back – this time hopefully it is not so loud.

Again, negative volume down, positive sound and vision up. How does this feel? Repeat this a few times to the point where the negative voice is hardly audible. This is a very simple but hugely powerful way of refocusing your habitual thought patterns and transforming them from negative and limiting to positive and affirming. Do this every day for the next nine days. Get into the habit of changing your habits.

Notes:

Day 55

New days, new ways

The greatest glory in living lies not in never falling, but in rising every time we fall.

Nelson Mandela

It is a simple yet profound truth that every day offers the possibility to renew and refresh. In Buddhism the day is a twenty-four hour reflection of the dynamic changes that occur throughout the lifetime of an individual as well as being a model for life at a micro and macro level. These four stages of change are birth, development, decay and death.

Approaching each day as new and a fresh opportunity to create a new life, new habits and to challenge our fears and past failings is central to this book. A day well lived could look like this:

- On waking (birth) we forget the failings and frustrations as well as the ego-feeding successes of yesterday and face the day ready to challenge, learn and create value for ourselves, others and the world.

- We act with wisdom and passion during the day (development), putting 100 per cent into what we do and who we are with. No backward-looking resentment or forward-facing fears.

- As the day draws to a close, so does our energy (decay) and we spend some time in quiet reflection or social time, maybe over a nice meal and a glass of wine with people we love, pondering the day and planning for tomorrow.

- Finally, we retire to bed, exhausted but content and we fall into a deep and refreshing sleep (death), where we regenerate ourselves ready for the new day ahead.

A life well lived is the combination of days embraced with courage, passion and love.

Live today as if it were your last

Repeat this conscious awareness of the cycle of birth, development, decay and death for the next few days (at least three). Each day until the end of the Enterprise section (Day 65), focus on this process. Try not to fill your mind with chatter and become overly concerned about what you should have done or anxious about achieving all your tasks in this short day. Do what you have to do with energy and gratitude. At the end of the day, jot down your thoughts on how the day went and how you felt. At the end of this section reread what you have written.

Notes:

Exercises throughout this section ◇

Linking the present to the future
Future focus
Live today as if it were your last

Exercises throughout the book

Wake up with gratitude
and vision
Meditation
Ask for help
Tune into your body
Review your goals
Be actively more supportive

Day 56

Motivation techniques

The secret to productive goal setting is establishing clearly defined goals, writing them down and then focusing on them several times a day with words and emotions as if we've already achieved them.

Denis Waitley

Once there was a donkey that was very stubborn. No matter how much the farmer who owned him shouted, pulled, pushed or beat him, if the donkey decided to stand still, he would. One day, on the road to the weekly market to sell vegetables, the donkey decided to stop. After an hour of shouting, pulling, beating and pleading, the donkey was still immobile and the farmer was worried that his vegetables would never get to market and he would not get any money for all his efforts.

The farmer had an idea. It was such a simple idea he was amazed that he had never thought of it before. He picked up the long stick that he had used to beat the stubborn donkey and tied a fat and succulent carrot to one end. Having positioned himself back on the cart he dangled the carrot just in front of the donkey. Now the donkey liked a carrot and stepped forward to take a bite. But as he moved so did the carrot. He took another step and then another until finally the donkey had walked all the way to the market.

After unpacking all the vegetables the farmer gave the carrot to the donkey who gobbled it down with satisfied crunches. The vegetables were all sold except for one. A carrot. The farmer had kept this to one side. How else was he to get home?

There is much to gain from a good yarn and this short story is no exception. One thing that we get from this tale is how often we behave like that donkey. Do we place our motivation on future reward by always striving towards what might be and never appreciating what is? What about just enjoying where we are? However challenging now might be it is going to change, so why not deal with the reality of it by drawing from the satisfaction of a new tomorrow? Do not wait for your world to give you a reason; be happy just for the hell of it.

Happiness for no good reason

Several times over the past fifty-five days you have been encouraged to try being grateful, being still, visualising, reflecting, taking action as well as numerous other strategies. This activity brings many of these suggestions into one.

In your daily meditations, focus on something specific that you want to achieve and visualise yourself achieving it. How would you feel in that glorious future? Draw that future feeling into the present. Like the carrot waving temptingly in front of the donkey, your happiness can be something that you will get one day.

Stop postponing your joy. Even if you haven't attained the literal gain you can experience the emotional satisfaction of attainment. Bathe yourself in this feeling of success, love or relief. Repeat this process daily until the end of the 101 days. You can do this whenever and wherever you are.

This conscious owning of your positive emotions will, over time, create a disposition of positive self-regard. This mindset is both fulfilling for oneself and attractive to others. Note how much quicker and more easily you attain your goals with this engagement in the fulfilment of the present. We are not totally sure how this works; we just know, after nearly thirty years of application, that it does.

Notes:

Exercises throughout this section ◇   Exercises throughout the book
Linking the present to the future   Wake up with gratitude
Future focus   and vision
Live today as if it were your last   Meditation
                                                            Ask for help
                                                      Tune into your body
                                                      Review your goals
                                                Be actively more supportive
                                                Happiness for no good reason

---

Day 57

Review your goals: Are they SMART?

Consistent physical structures can allow unbounded intuitive clarity.

Mary Anne Radmacher

Anyone who has been around management processes since the early eighties will know the technique that we are about to share with you. The reason it works, and why it is therefore worth including in this guide to managing change, is that it breaks any task into clear and accessible chunks.

There is nothing mysterious about it – it just makes sense. The reasons why people fail in applying this technique are many and varied but are usually linked with lack of self-belief. Hopefully by now you are seeing the small but significant improvements in your own life that mean that the introduction (or reminder) of this process will provide you with another tool for transformation.

Sometimes it's the most apparently boring and uncreative processes that can lead to great breakthroughs and innovative thinking. Always seeking the rush of creativity without having a framework for that creative flow to follow can often lead to a feeling of drowning in too many possibilities. Below is an exercise that will provide some steer to your genius.

SMART thinking

SMART has been given several meanings over the years but the ones that work well for us are:

- **S**pecific – be clear about what you want to achieve; vagueness will mean you'll lose focus.

- **M**anageable – make sure you can manage this new challenge. Are your circumstances right or do you need to apply a little SMART thinking to other things first before you can take on any fresh goals?

- **A**chievable – are you being overly confident or naive about being able to achieve this goal? If not, rethink and then start the SMART process with a fresh and more tangible objective.

- **R**ealistic – are you being optimistic about the outcomes or does this goal fall within the realms of reality?

- **T**ime sensitive – set yourself a timeframe to achieve this goal. If it is a grand plan then break your plan down into small chunks of time, reflecting and amending the SMART goals as you go along.

Get your journal out and set yourself a new goal or look at those you've set yourself already. It can be anything from something you'd like to achieve in a couple of days or at the end of this 101-day process. Apply some SMART thinking to your goals and take the action you need to move your life forward to where you know it can be.

Notes:

Day 58

Overcoming obstacles

Courage is going from failure to failure
without losing your enthusiasm.

Winston Churchill

We hope by now you have failed at some of the tasks you have set yourself. Maybe you have not done what you set out to do or you have tried hard but someone else has let you down. Maybe you feel overwhelmed at what you feel is necessary to shatter the negative habits that have built up – or you are perhaps irritated by the smug, self-satisfied and sanctimonious tone of this book! Whatever your reason for wanting to stop, whatever the obstacle that is facing you now, see it for what it is: inevitable.

The writing of this book has been, for all three of us, a real challenge. We have no intention of presenting examples of how we've all had to dig deep for the ideas that we are sharing with you; this book is about supporting you rather than a vehicle for highlighting our personal challenges and victories. We just wanted to share with you that the success of writing it has been built on moving from failure to failure without losing enthusiasm for the task.

We all need to grasp the fact that failure is an inevitable part of the process of change. To expect perfection and constant success in all things is unreasonable, unworkable and unobtainable. We sincerely want you to enjoy the rewards that will come by applying some of the techniques we are sharing, but we don't expect that you'll succeed in everything. Just take one step each day, even if sometimes you find yourself taking a few backward ones along the way. Not being perfect is just part of the dynamic of life.

Starting afresh

If you have been keeping a journal, look back through the entries and choose an exercise or a day when you tried something and it didn't work out or you wanted to try something and didn't get round to it. Start again. Have another attempt. Once you've given it a go, pop your thoughts and feelings down in your journal. If you haven't been keeping a journal then start one today.

If you are picking up this book at random, go to Day 1 and make a commitment to read the first section on Survival. You can continue through the rest of the book if you like, but try to stick to something without distraction for a couple of weeks. Once you've done that, reflect on how it felt and, if it was a rewarding experience, commit to go through the second section. Repeat this process until you have finished the whole book.

Today's exercise: Starting afresh

Notes:

Day 59

What are my incentives?

Most people never run far enough on their first wind to find out they've got a second. Give your dreams all you've got and you'll be amazed at the energy that comes out of you.

William James

What makes you keep going? When things get tough, does your determination waver? One way to provide a litmus test for your incentives is to understand that the decisions that you make are no more than a manifestation of the values that you hold. On Day 27 we discussed this and gave an exercise for you to clarify your values and to reflect on whether you lived your values or just had them.

Values and drives may alter or adjust as your circumstances and existential challenges change. It is therefore very important, if you are to keep yourself going, to have a clear idea of what your values are. Sometimes, in order to assess where we are and what we are doing or need to do, it is worth stepping away from our endeavours and looking back on our lives as a critical friend. Of course you could just go to your critical friends and family and ask them, but today we would like to share a technique that draws on several exercises you have been exposed to thus far. If you are just playing 'flip the page open and let fate decide' then this will work for you as well.

For some, the thing that gives them greatest incentive to act is a higher purpose or even a higher power. A great goal or even a mission can provide us with the drive to overcome any immediate setbacks.

Dear ...

Try this exercise (which was inspired by Lesley Garner's *Everything I've Ever Done that Worked*) as a challenge to your openness and creativity. Sit down with your journal and write a letter beginning: 'Dear ...' Then write, without thinking about it too much, whatever situation or problem you'd like help with. Then sign it 'Yours gratefully (your own name)'. Now, without stopping to think, write a reply straight back. 'Dear (your name), This is how I see your situation. This is what I think you should do ... Yours, ever, ...' Reflect upon the answer you provide yourself, or that has been channelled to you, and then take one action today to challenge the situation or problem that you wrote about.

Today's exercise: Dear ...

Notes:

Day 60

Imagining success: Three months from now ...

The key question of the 21st century is not whether you are on the left or on the right, but whether you are open or closed. This applies to nations, firms, institutions and individuals. To be closed is simple and perhaps a visceral human reaction. To be open is a much greater challenge.

Jean-Pierre Lehmann

What is the point of dreaming? Where is the value in imagining a future that is positive, fruitful and peaceful? Surely our focus is engaging with the present and dealing with the demands of today! But too much of one can lead to an imbalance of energy. Pouring all our efforts into today with no vision for the future can create frustration and fatigue. Too much planning and hoping for the future can lead to procrastination and an inability to build on the potential of each day. We need both if we are going to create a dynamic balance between engaging with the present while moving towards the future.

The power of creative visualisation has been referred to several times over the past sixty days and there is a simple reason why – it works. Dreaming has become, through millions of years of evolution, a central part of our existence. The fact that dreaming and visualisation are so central to healthy brain function is an indication that it not only has a purpose but also will evolve further with the right discipline and attention.

Today we want to share another technique that will assist you in a very practical way to draw your future success towards you.

Future thoughts

Put yourself into a relaxed state using the techniques in previous exercises, and choose a clear goal three months from now – it could be to feel fitter, have better relationships with your family or work colleagues, anything.

Visualise yourself three months hence having achieved your goal. You may want to use your journal to draw a mind-map or write down key words or descriptions of what you see and how you feel. Or you can just imagine it. When you attain your goal, who are you with and what are you saying? Create a very positive, multisensory image of where you want to be. Allow the waves of satisfaction, love, achievement and relief at a job well done to wash over you.

Visualise a path from where you are focusing in the future to where you are now. The path can be straight or winding, tarmacked or a woodland trail. You decide. Now, imagine this path as a timeline, with the now where you are right at this moment and the three months concluding at the end of the path. Now come back down the path two weeks from the imagined endpoint. Where do you need to be on your path in order for you to succeed on your journey? You might imagine yourself having a romantic and positive meal with your partner or having cleared out the garage ready to put in that mini-gym. Be clear where you need to be and imagine yourself there. Again, go through all of the senses to make the image as powerful as possible.

Come back down the path by another two weeks. Repeat the process. Then another two weeks, and another, and another. Now visualise yourself at the end of tomorrow. What do you need to have done by the end of tomorrow to be on track to get to where you need to be in two weeks time?

If when you do this process you realise that your ambitions were either unclear or unrealistic, then adjust your vision to make it more SMART (see Day 57).

This balance between clarity of direction via logistics and cultivating a strong will – in a way that we don't fully understand but have experienced many times – combines to draw that outcome towards you.

Today's exercise: Future thoughts

Notes:

Day 61

Honing my actions

Success is the sum of small efforts
repeated day in and day out.

Robert Collier

Hopefully by now you have begun to create a daily habit of picking up this book and applying some of the exercises. If not, in these last forty days we want to encourage you to really challenge yourself to discover the creativity, insights and mastery that can come through the repetition of small everyday efforts.

In her book *Leadership and the New Science*, Margaret Wheatley looks at how our growing understanding of nature and science reveals an underlying 'self organising' system that pervades the whole universe. When we model these simple but profound laws in our own lives and organisations our relationships will become more open and our productivity will be raised to unexpected levels.

Central to this success is to bring a little chaos into the equation. Chaos, as defined by Timothy Cartwright, is 'order without predictability'. Dynamic and creative growth requires that we abide by central principles, values or processes and allow new ideas and relationships to develop through repetition.

Another example of this is the practice of Tai Chi, which explores a series of movements to generate well-being and physical, emotional and spiritual growth. The moves are always the same but by deepening our awareness and adding subtle improvements to the techniques we can master this art more fully.

What in your life are you consciously repeating, deepening and expanding your understanding of? Is every day so unbounded that the effort and insights released evaporate due to lack of basic structures or systems?

A little and often

Look at your journal entries from Day 1 and see if there is a recurring theme or issue. Is there an aspect of your life that you really want to shift, once and for all? Whatever it is, write it down. You may well have made that commitment and could be challenging this every day; if so, this is going to be a reminder. If not, then this is the start of your journey.

Every day from now until Day 101 repeat a simple task, mantra or exercise so that it becomes a habit. It could be to do with improving your morning meditations or something that you want to enhance regarding your relationships with others. It could be about taking regular exercise or having time to read to your children. Whatever it is, do this every day. Review the impact of this in forty days when you complete the final challenge of this book.

Notes:

Exercises throughout this section ◇

Linking the present to the future
Future focus
Live today as if it were your last
SMART thinking

Exercises throughout the book

Wake up with gratitude
and vision
Meditation
Ask for help
Tune into your body
Review your goals
Be actively more supportive
Happiness for no good reason
A little and often

Day 62

Clarity of purpose: Finding your mantra

A man is a success if he gets up in the morning and goes to bed at night and in between does what he wants to do.

Bob Dylan

Yesterday we used the term 'mantra'. Let's look a little deeper at how mantras can help or hinder your happiness and success. What mantras do you already have that are either lifting you up or bringing you down? What are you saying over and over to yourself that is adding to your success or blocking your happiness?

This inner voice can be the difference between success and failure. We all lack confidence. Each of us has at least two voices in our head. One voice is saying that you are great, gifted and more than capable. The other voice is saying today is the day that they find you out. The trick, and it is a trick, is to turn up the positive and turn off the negative.

We looked at turning the volume down on our negatives on Day 54. Today we want to share with you another technique to embed the positive voice of confidence even deeper. This is confidence; not arrogance. The difference between the two is this: confident people give you energy and arrogant people seek to steal it from you in order to fill their own void within. We'll examine this theory more deeply later on in the book (see Day 68).

Write it down

Open your journal and review the thoughts of the past few days and then write down how you will feel on Day 101 once you have successfully reached any of your goals. Begin the sentence: 'By Day 101, I will feel ...' Then rewrite the sentence: 'Today I will feel ...' Then rewrite it again: 'I feel ...'

No postponement or delaying your joy. 'I feel ...' is a choice. Every day write that sentence at the beginning of your journal entry. Use the techniques that you have been exposed to in order to embed that emotional response. Hold on to that feeling and get on with your day.

At the end of the day, write it down again and consciously create that state of positive self-regard before you sleep.

> Notes:

Exercises throughout this section ◇ Exercises throughout the book

Linking the present to the future	Wake up with gratitude and vision
Future focus	Meditation
Live today as if it were your last	Ask for help
SMART thinking	Tune into your body
	Review your goals
	Be actively more supportive
	Happiness for no good reason
	A little and often
	Write it down

Day 63

Stop!

I long to accomplish a great and noble task,
but it is my chief duty to accomplish small tasks as
if they were great and noble.

Helen Keller

Sometimes we put so much energy into working towards a big goal we can overlook the opportunities to make a difference to where we are now. Indeed, the capacity to manage each task, however menial and apparently unimportant, is the pathway to accomplishing a more lofty dream.

Each day presents us with numerous moments to make a difference to our lives, the lives of others and the world. However, if we have got into the deluded mindset that our happiness and purpose on earth is at the end of some imagined journey, we run the risk of missing out on so much joy, adventure and amazement that can be found in the mundane.

One of the other dangers of allowing the feelings of worth, joy and satisfaction to appear only once we have completed our goal is that much of our lives will be full of dissatisfaction and struggle. The following exercise is designed to remind you of the importance of seizing the joy within your grasp.

Today's exercise

Watch a movie

Stopping once in a while and celebrating mundane joys is what this exercise is all about. On your own or with a friend, family members or lover, hire two films from two distinct genres. One should be fun, a comedy or adventure, and the other a more philosophical, poignant or art house film. Maybe come up with a list and then get your co-viewers to choose. Get in food, treats and wine (if appropriate) – invest some time in making the detail of the environment important.

If you have invited guests, look for small things to celebrate when they arrive. Say thank you to them for making time to spend the evening with you. Comment on how important your relationship with them is. Compliment them for their choice in shoes! Zoom in on the little things and make them huge. Snuggle down, get comfy. Eat, drink and enjoy the movies. Talk and see how the evening goes.

This is not merely an indulgent pleasure: it's an important pit stop of love for you just to take stock of all that you have.

Today's exercise: Watch a movie

Notes:

Day 64

Visions and dreams

*The most beautiful thing we can experience is the
mysterious. It is the source of all true art and all science.
He to whom this emotion is a stranger... is as good as dead:
his eyes are closed.*

Albert Einstein

On Day 60 we looked at how dreaming and visioning could assist you to draw your success closer to you. Dreams are incredibly powerful and, to really embed deep thinking and profound belief systems, getting your subconscious involved is a dynamic way of cementing personal confidence.

How often have you gone to bed and tried to sleep only to be kept awake by the negative thoughts, imagined disagreements and overly anxious concerns about what you have or haven't done? When we harness our imagination we can not only improve our sleeping patterns but use our rest as a means of hard-wiring our dreams into beliefs so that our actions become that much more powerful.

The following exercise is about trusting your intuition. Most of us have been educated *not* to listen to our inner voice and regard intuition as a bit fluffy. However, when you begin to realise that gut reaction (and not ego-driven illusion) is a powerful and helpful tool, it will be something that you'll want to put time and effort into rediscovering and refining.

Pillow talk

Take your journal to bed. In addition to any other end-of-day scribbling, write a question or concern that might otherwise keep you awake or that you just want to challenge and solve. For example, 'How do I keep reading this book and take action right until the last day?' Use one of the relaxation and/or positive visualisation techniques you have been shown and put yourself into a deep sleep.

On waking read the question and write down an answer. Whatever it is, just write it down. You might even wake up with a person on your mind. Write their name down. If you have a dream, write down as much as you can remember. Return to it and reflect on the images. Do this for the next ten days and then reflect on what you have dreamt about to see how you feel now and if you need to take some action. Act intuitively and see where this leads. Sound weird? Don't let that stop you!

Notes:

Exercises throughout this section   ◇
Linking the present to the future
Future focus
Live today as if it were your last
SMART thinking
Pillow talk

Exercises throughout the book
Wake up with gratitude
and vision
Meditation
Ask for help
Tune into your body
Review your goals
Be actively more supportive
Happiness for no good reason
A little and often
Write it down

Day 65

See yourself in action

*Only as high as I reach can I grow, only as far as
I seek can I go, only as deep as I look can I see, only
as much as I dream can I be.*

Karen Ravn

Everything about who you are is a habit and the activities you have been doing over these past days have been assisting you to consciously challenge any limiting beliefs and choose the 'you' you wish to be.

While some of the exercises have been very much focused on where you are going and what things are going to look like when you get there, much can be gained by just daydreaming. For many serious-minded, thinking individuals the idea of daydreaming is a waste of time. If that is your knee-jerk reaction, give yourself the chance to be open to a different way of thinking.

Dreaming has many positive physical and emotional benefits. It feeds some decent chemicals into our brains, lifts our spirits and gives us joy.

Today, as the last day in this section on Enterprise, we want you to dream for dreaming's sake. No big outcomes or worthy tasks; just liberate yourself from reality for a while.

Today's exercise

Dream time

Put yourself into a relaxed state and look through the positive filing system of your brain. You could choose to go backwards

– skimming the happy, fun and delightful memories of your recent or distant past – or scan forwards to the imagined joys and excitement of the future. Whenever you come across a memory or dream that delights you, rest there. Explore it. Draw joy from it, then either move on or change direction.

Do this for a while until you are all topped up with good feelings. There is no time limit – two minutes or two hours. Just have fun and indulge yourself in your imagination and get happy.

Today's exercise: Dream time

Notes:

Exercises throughout this section ◇   Exercises throughout the book

Linking the present to the future   Wake up with gratitude
Future focus   and vision
Live today as if it were your last   Meditation
SMART thinking   Ask for help
Pillow talk   Tune into your body
Review your goals
Be actively more supportive
Happiness for no good reason
A little and often
Write it down

Section 6

Community

How Do I Deepen My Relationships and Build Bonds?

Day 66

Inspiring people:
Letting them guide me

Keep away from people who try to belittle your ambitions.
Small people always do that, but the really great make you
feel that you, too, can become great.

Mark Twain

We are influenced and affected by those around us on a daily basis. Some of us pay greater heed than others to the power other people exert over them. If we grew up with very authoritarian parents then perhaps we automatically kowtow to those in high places, or the pendulum may have swung the other way and we tend to rebel against or mistrust those who seem to have higher status than us. As stated earlier, there's a saying that confident people give us energy, arrogant people seek to steal it. In other words, someone who is stable and at ease with themselves and their gifts and abilities wants to share that sensation to create a more positive atmosphere wherever they go, whereas those who feel insecure and threatened by anyone happier/more successful/richer/cleverer than them seek to make others feel smaller in their presence to fill that deep lack within. We are all familiar with both types of people, and as Mark Twain's quote suggests, it's important to try to surround yourself with people who care enough to seek to help you grow in autonomy and to become the most effective you can be.

There are people in our lives who we feel drawn to because they possess something that we aspire to or they simply set us an example by the way they choose to live. Remember, it's not about comparison – *judging* ourselves in the context of others is profoundly unhelpful and ultimately damaging. If we choose to be competitive, there will always be people, wherever we get to in our lives, who seem to be doing better than us and conversely, those who are not doing as well. So try not to fall into that trap – this is about how others can inspire us to concentrate on what is unique about us so that it can be nurtured. It may be that they possess a particular skill or attribute that they have tended and allowed to flourish; perhaps they have an ease about them or they seem to know exactly who they are and how they fit into the world. People who have developed a gift or are comfortable in their own skin are magnetic to be around – they remind us of what is possible. We *all* have untapped potential and those we are drawn to have invested in their own in a way that can really motivate us.

Today's exercise

Inspiring qualities

Building on an earlier exercise (Day 52), think about those people in your life who have inspired you or motivated you to be more yourself. They may be alive or dead, they may be familiar to you (e.g. part of your family, circle of friends, partner) or key figures in history, the arts, science and so on. Identify and write down the qualities you feel they possess. Ask yourself, what is it about that person that creates awe, wonder or positivity in me?

In a second list, think about what aspects of yourself you would like to develop or explore in light of this. What potential qualities within would you like to focus on? How can you begin to do this seriously?

Today's exercise: Inspiring qualities

Notes:

Day 67

Who has helped me in my life and how?

There is hope in people. Not systems,
or governments; people.

Anon.

Sometimes when we are going through dark or complex times, we can feel completely isolated and disconnected from those around us. We may convince ourselves that we are destined to remain ultimately separate and unknowable from the people in our lives. This can result in an inability to see or hear what others are willing to offer us in the way of advice, companionship and care. We may also be looking for grand solutions to our problems when in fact we can learn so much from the quieter messages from those around us.

Think back to those who have helped you in your life. It may be obvious acts of generosity by your parents, for example, contributing to the costs of your education – it may only be with hindsight that you realise just how much they were willing to sacrifice for your future. Or it may be a teacher – a particular lesson that inspired us to learn because it was so stimulating and enjoyable. Maybe a friend or a relative made a special effort to help us find a way forward with a problem or a practical issue – they may have offered us a place to stay while we worked out our next move. Perhaps a work colleague told us about a particular opportunity that gave our career a boost.

Sometimes we vividly remember a few words from someone that had a profound effect on our lives – a piece of counsel or advice that we instinctively knew was worth listening to because it came from someone's valuable experience. It may even have led us to change direction. Somehow we understood that they were passing it on to us because they genuinely wanted us to learn from their mistakes and successes.

The humblest moments in a day can ultimately be life changing. The best-selling author Caroline Myss (1997) tells a story about a desperately depressed and suicidal young man who absent-mindedly stepped out in front of a woman's car; she astounded him by looking directly into his eyes and smiling warmly at him. That moment changed his life – he realised that we all have a choice to connect with those around us, and he chose to live. Just that one moment of humanity was the difference between life and death for him. These small, humble actions can have a huge impact on us.

Today's exercise

Help from our friends

Set some time aside to consider the people who have helped you in your life, through their words and actions. Write down their names and acknowledge with gratitude their contribution to making you who you are today. How did they affect you? What did you do differently because of what they said to you? Consider how you can pay this forward. What can you pass on to others? How can your experience be of use to those around you? How can you build bridges with the people you encounter in your life?

Today's exercise: Help from our friends

Notes:

Day 68

Staying open, avoiding pride

No man is an island entire of itself; every man is a piece of the continent, a part of the main.

John Donne

If you recall on Day 62 we talked about the difference between confidence and arrogance and how the need to feel more important than those around us will always skew our behaviour. The energy it takes to continually exert superiority is exhausting and can lead to habitual feelings of discomfort and emptiness. Always trying to protect our ego from potential threats is a very frustrating and unpleasant way to live. We are ultimately struggling with our own insecurities or a sensation of lack that may date back to ancient wounds which have no bearing on the present or the people around us. The more we are able to distinguish between our ego and our higher selves – the part of us that yearns to be positive and constructive – the more fulfilling and loving our relationships with those around us will be. In our need to be top dog we can end up seeing others as separate or even hostile to our position and we are then unable to be loving towards them. It costs us so much not to turn off that instinct.

Pride is our downfall every time. The madness of pride is ultimately destructive – we are afraid that by surrendering to being kind or compassionate we will lose or give something up. If we can't see past the filter of our pride it really *does* become a jungle out there, where survival of the fittest is key. Try to look at life through the eyes of humility – not the fear of humiliation. It's our choice and one we can make every minute of our lives. We don't have to be slaves to our ego and our pride. We need to see other people as sacred beings too; otherwise we will try to find a way to be better than them.

Staying open to others means experiencing a deeper connection and a welcome relief from the tyranny of our ego. It means we can be witnessed in our authenticity and enjoy the wonderful freedom of developing a strong and honest bond with those around us.

Today's exercise

Letting go of ego

Think and write about the moments in your life when you experience a strong sensation (or spike) of jealousy or threat to your ego. Take time to connect with that sensation and think about when this happens. Who is it with? What are the circumstances? What can it tell you about yourself? Does this come from a past difficulty – a time when you were criticised or hurt? How can you allow this sensation to exist but pass on so that you don't suffer too much or react from it, or expend energy blaming the other person or yourself? What do you really want your relationships to be like? How can you stay open and constructive? What positive qualities in you are calling to be explored that are currently being suppressed?

Take time to write these things down and try to understand that these reactions are generated by *you* – therefore *you* have control over them. What can you do to turn them around?

Today's exercise: Letting go of ego

Notes:

Wearing someone else's boots

Love is everything it's cracked up to be. That's why people are so cynical about it. It really is worth fighting for, being brave for, risking everything for. And the trouble is, if you don't risk anything, you risk even more.

Erica Jong

We all long to be loving. Think about it: not being on your guard around others; putting energy into being open, giving and caring, rather than worrying about how we look or behave or are perceived; feeling understood, witnessed and relaxed to be ourselves because we trust that people are behaving with good intent and an open heart. Consider how you feel at those times when you are motivated to do something for someone other than yourself, just for the sake of giving. There's a sense of liberation and space within; we feel expansive and more at peace with ourselves. Why does this have to be a rare sensation?

In our sophisticated and cynical times we seem to have developed 'compassion fatigue' – a belief that it is weak and 'Hallmark Card' sentimental to be habitually kind and thoughtful. Have you noticed that when we do come across people who behave in this way, it's conspicuous by its unusual nature? Those rare moments when people who aren't in our close circle go out of their way to open a door, smile and say hello, give us a casual compliment and so on. What does this say about the way we live? Without resorting to Pollyanna-esque thinking, there is much that we can do on a daily basis to improve our lives with empathy and compassion for those around us. They don't have to be grand gestures; just thinking from another's perspective can be enlightening and hugely improve our relationships with our nearest and dearest as well as strangers.

What is true compassion? Some might say it recognises that the boundaries we perceive between ourselves and others are an illusion. This may seem unrealistic and beyond our desire, but we move closer to it every time we see past our own self-concern to accommodate others.

Extending ourselves by trying to understand other's points of view can help with the flow of our daily lives and deepen our relationships. Rather than having our own agenda uppermost, it can be helpful to see what another person's reality is and why that affects the way they behave. We all have different priorities and it's all too easy to get caught up in our own and consider them to be the most important all of the time.

Today's exercise

Random acts of kindness

Where appropriate, for the next seven days try to make an effort to tune in to the people around you and put yourself in their shoes. Embrace and enjoy the concept of planning some guerrilla-style random acts of kindness! How can you brighten someone else's day (and at the same time illuminate your own too)? It might be sending an email, picking up some shopping, smiling at a stranger, sending a card, inviting someone over for a meal, giving up your seat on the tube and so on. How do these experiences improve your life?

Notes:

Exercises throughout this section ◇ Exercises throughout the book

Random acts of kindness

Wake up with gratitude
and vision

Meditation

Ask for help

Tune into your body

Review your goals

Be actively more supportive

Happiness for no good reason

A little and often

Write it down

Day 70

How can I stay true to myself in a group?

*To free us from the expectations of others,
to give us back to ourselves – there lies the great,
singular power of self-respect.*

Joan Didion

Yesterday we focused on being more empathic towards others and remembering that freeing ourselves up to be more understanding will help to give our own lives increased meaning. Today we will look at maintaining healthy relationships from another angle – how to preserve our sense of self while remaining open to others.

We all exist as a single element within a variety of larger groups, both personally and professionally. Our family, our work colleagues, our social lives, a shared interest group – we are one of a number, and we have a responsibility to those around us for these groups to function with a degree of harmony. We are required to take on board other people's opinions and to accommodate their feelings and points of view. Some of us, however, feel a sense of duty to others over ourselves and we can inadvertently end up giving ourselves away. Our reflexive action can be to agree with others, whether it's for a quieter life or to achieve consensus.

Just as with self-sabotaging (see Day 33), sometimes the need to feel liked, to be compliant or to simply not rock the boat can take precedence over our truest response to a situation. We may enjoy feeling part of a collaborative group but if we allow our need to be accepted to override our integrity we are essentially selling ourselves short and not serving the situation or ultimately the people we are with. To qualify: this isn't about selfishness or getting our own way; it's about honesty and clarity so that we are an effective and active member of a group. It's also about being consistently authentic within every context of our lives – trying not to bend ourselves out of shape to make sure we fit in with all the environments of which we are a part.

When it comes to making group-based decisions our responsibility – literally, our ability to respond – needs to be to ourselves just as much as to others. If we go against our own grain, or at the very least push down a rising instinct and don't voice it, then we ultimately are the ones who end up suffering. We lose a little bit of self-respect and autonomy. Over time, we can forget that we are a separate entity (particularly if the group in question has a few louder voices) and neglect to check in with ourselves.

Today's exercise

Staying authentic

Consider the impact you have within the various groups of which you are a part – at work, at home, socially. Are you able to remain true to yourself while holding other people's points of view? Do you feel that you represent yourself when decisions are being made or do you hold back your opinion? Are there times when you suppress a desire to contribute as you know your comments might put the spotlight on you and make you feel uncomfortable? How many hats do you wear and does this affect how you present yourself to various people? Write down your thoughts and reactions in your journal.

Today's exercise: Staying authentic

Notes:

Day 71

Healing the hurt: Do I want to feel bitter or better?

It is by going down into the abyss that we recover the treasures of life. Where you stumble, there lies your treasure.

Joseph Campbell

None of us manage to sail through life unscathed by fall-outs or misunderstandings with others. More often than not these disagreements happen with family members with whom we don't choose to have a relationship. But whether it's family or friends we have a problem with, if we fail to fully address difficulties at the time they happen we are in danger of being stuck with the residue of something far more damaging in the long run. Unresolved issues that stay untended can create a toxic block that brings us up short every time we think of that particular person or event and ultimately compromises our relationships with others. Areas that we can't discuss or that become taboo mean we are not fully present with that person and are marooned somewhere in the past.

Some of us may know people who have gone a step further and no longer have contact with key members of their family or friendship group – people that they were once very close to or had a strong bond with. Sadly, it's sometimes far easier to let a situation fester or slide and before we know it, the root of the problem is almost irrelevant; we are just left with a sense of resentment or anger that still packs the power of the original punch. Re-establishing a relationship then becomes awkward, painful and challenging.

Of course, life is complicated. We can't always get back to how things once were and sometimes we outgrow people; our situations change and we lose touch for a reason. However, cutting a significant person out of our lives can be a terrible loss.

Even if we decide not to reconnect or we have accepted that a relationship has changed over time, it's wise to check in with ourselves to acknowledge our part in the dynamic and to let go of any feelings of recrimination or resentment. Otherwise we may continue to have imaginary conversations with the person in question and build up more negativity around the situation. If we are saddled with those unpleasant feelings, ultimately we are the ones who suffer.

Today's exercise

Dealing with disagreement

Focus on a relationship where there is a lack of clarity or some unresolved issues that affect your communication with that person. Write down exactly how you feel and why, allowing any feelings of anger, sadness or frustration to be expressed. Once you've nothing left to say, write a letter to the person concerned. Try to be honest and clear, as well as accountable, when it comes to your part in the problem. Attempt to be constructive and positive where possible. When you have finished the letter you may choose to send it or not; the act of writing it is the most important element as you will have allowed yourself to explore a painful sensation. Note down how you feel after the exercise. Has anything shifted within? Do you feel more at peace with the situation? Why?

Today's exercise: Dealing with disagreement

Notes:

Day 72

Forgiveness

True forgiveness is a self-healing process which starts with
you and gradually extends to everyone else.

Robert Holden

Following on from yesterday, we are going to focus on the concept of forgiveness. Real forgiveness, which must come from the most authentic part of ourselves, takes patience and commitment but will ultimately give us peace of mind and freedom to move forward with self-confidence and renewed purpose. It will also improve the quality of our relationships by giving us greater insight into the way we relate to others.

According to psychologist and therapist Dr Fred Luskin, author of *Forgive for Good*, the simple definition of forgiveness is 'the ability to make peace with the word "no"?'.

By that he means accepting there is little point in fighting against people or events that thwart your expectations or fly in the face of your ambitions or sense of justice. Certain things are beyond our control: an unfaithful partner, an unloving parent, a traumatic betrayal. It's only natural that we find the concept of forgiveness hard to swallow when we feel we've been especially wronged. We might want some sort of comeback or even revenge. The last thing we may feel like doing is forgiving the perpetrator because by doing so we feel we're saying, 'It's OK, it doesn't matter. I'm letting you off the hook.' This is the stumbling block for many of us.

But forgiveness isn't necessarily about skipping off into the sunset with the person who hurt you or condoning their actions. It's about acknowledging that distress, anger or hurt feelings are damaging for us and our progress, so there's little point in hanging on to them. Of course, those feelings need to be expressed – whether to a trusted friend or, if appropriate, to the person in question. But the key is getting a realistic perspective on the event and transforming your emotional response to it. Only then can you turn your gaze outward and feel released enough to engage with the people in your life that it would be beneficial for you to forgive. Only then will you stop replaying the incident and hurting yourself each time.

Today's exercise

Moving on from hurt

Focus on a situation where you felt compromised, let down or hurt by someone. Acknowledge that it would be helpful for your well-being to find a way to extend forgiveness to the person/ people involved, but first you need to truly acknowledge your own feelings.

Find a comfortable position, close your eyes and put attention on your breathing. Allow your body to fully relax. While deepening your breath and quietening your mind, think about the situation and open yourself up to your feelings. Try not to judge or criticise yourself in the process or to escape from the hurt. Sit with the sensations until they have passed. Try to feel compassion for yourself that you still suffer from the effects of what happened. Ask yourself how you can turn this around, so that you can be released from the grip of what happened. Do you want to stay locked in with this feeling? What is it you need to do? How can you express what you need to say? Can you write this down? Respect yourself enough to know that there are other options in terms of how you choose to feel. Obviously, you cannot change the past, but ask yourself how you would like to continue in the face of this experience.

Today's exercise: Moving on from hurt

Notes:

Exercises throughout this section ◇
Random acts of kindness

Exercises throughout the book
Wake up with gratitude
and vision
Meditation
Ask for help
Tune into your body
Review your goals
Be actively more supportive
Happiness for no good reason
A little and often
Write it down

Day 73

Improving my relationships

True friends stab you in the front.

Oscar Wilde

Friendship is a strong and habitual inclination in two persons to promote the good and happiness of one another.

Eustace Budgell

Sometimes we need to do a health check when it comes to the quality of our relationships. Many of us automatically put a lot of energy into our personal lives and making sure our intimate relationships are in good working order, but we are less accountable when it comes to dynamics with our friends and colleagues. Admittedly, bringing our whole selves to work is a challenge and not always appropriate, but having a consistent set of values when it comes to those with whom we choose to associate and keeping integrity in our professional dealings requires a level of autonomy that it is our duty to develop. It also means we are operating from a place of good intention because we are choosing to take responsibility for our behaviour. This can only serve us well in the long run and help us to respect ourselves and value our relationships.

Our well-being can be easily influenced by those around us. Do the people you choose to spend the most time with enrich and add something to your life or do they exhaust your resources? Are there people that you feel duty-bound to support while you get nothing back from them or who sap your energy with their constant griping, gossiping or negativity? Conversely, there may be friends who seem willing to be a sounding board for you but are reluctant to share the deeper part of themselves – who aren't inclined to meet you in the middle. Perhaps it's time to redress the balance and to challenge these dynamics by being honest about how you feel or choosing to spend less time with certain people. While this may involve making some initially uncomfortable changes to our social lives, it can bring about an empowering transformation which comes from being true to oneself. We can also gain much from choosing to acknowledge to a person how precious their friendship is to us. Don't hold back or wait until it's too late to tell someone how much you care about them. Our relationships can flourish and grow on the basis of such candour.

Invest in meaningful relationships

Over the next few days, find time to focus on how you can invest in, improve and clarify the meaningful relationships in your life. Consider the people who contribute to your well-being through their friendship, understanding or support, or whose values match your own. Identify what each person brings to your life. Do you spend enough time with these people? Think of ways you can invest more quality time in being with them. Think about those people you care about who may need extra support right now. What can you realistically offer them? It's also useful to identify those people you feel compromised by or unable to be yourself around. How can you be more honest with them? Ask yourself if you are prepared to do what is necessary to live all your relationships in a more truthful and fulfilling way. Write down your thoughts and reactions in your journal.

Notes:

Exercises throughout this section ◇   Exercises throughout the book

Random acts of kindness

Invest in meaningful
relationships

Wake up with gratitude
and vision

Meditation

Ask for help

Tune into your body

Review your goals

Be actively more supportive

Happiness for no good reason

A little and often

Write it down

Day 74

Making a difference

From what we get, we can make a living;
what we give, however, makes a life.

Arthur Ashe

A key part of our evolution and development is the need to be of service. This isn't to do with being worthy or submitting ourselves to martyrdom. It's about freeing ourselves from the concerns of our ego and the pursuit of our own progress, and finding ways to be of use to those around us or even to contribute to the wider world. We exist as part of a whole and it's through our deeds and intentions that we stay truly connected. The old adage suggests that giving feels better than receiving – that experience of inner expansiveness already discussed in this book. It's what makes people donate to charity or to disaster relief funds. It brings us out of ourselves and into the wider world, ready and willing to lend a hand to those in need. When we respond to a call to action in this way we may feel as if we are finally doing something really important, and this can lead us to feel more substantial and authentic. Some may argue that this in itself is a selfish act; that ultimately we are making ourselves feel better through these so-called altruistic deeds. What can't possibly be disputed is that the net result is positive from any angle!

As we continue to expand beyond a self-involved perspective, a seismic shift can take place in our reality. We will find that it's much easier to be happy when we are motivated in tangible ways to make the world a more loving place – by responding to the call of those who are suffering or who are simply in need. Sometimes it's easier, of course, to respond to a high-profile catastrophic event rather than focusing on ongoing problems like homelessness, poverty and illness, or even less obvious issues such as isolation and loneliness. But the more we promote, applaud and actively inspire humanitarian efforts in the world, the more others will be drawn to this kind of work. We can be an example in the way that we choose to give of ourselves.

Today's exercise

Giving of yourself

Make time to reflect on what you can do to be of service in your community, workplace or society. Is there anything that you feel inspired or called to do? What skills do you have that may be useful? Could you volunteer spare time to an organisation that you feel is worthwhile? Or if you don't have a great deal of time to offer, are there things you can donate? Perhaps there's something you can do that's closer to home, in terms of the people who live in your neighbourhood. The reward that comes from investing efforts in the well-being of those around us is extremely satisfying. Write down your thoughts and reactions in your trusty journal.

Today's exercise: Giving of yourself

Notes:

Day 75

Grace in action:
A growthful choice

Respect is love in plain clothes.

Frankie Byrne

Every day we are presented with a myriad of options in terms of our interactions with others. If we walk around reacting unconsciously, our dynamics with the people we encounter are likely to be unremarkable and without much significance. You may argue that time is always against us – we don't have the luxury of being able to chat in depth about meaningful matters with everyone we meet, and why would we want to? Of course the pace and complexity of life dictates our actions, and we can't develop deep bonds with everyone, but at every moment, however fleeting, we have the power to decide how we choose to behave around others and to make our exchanges constructive. Each interaction can be unique and satisfying in a different way. We can choose to come from a place of grace and compassion, or not. Either we decide to trust and respect the people we are faced with, or not.

Think back over the past few days and try to recall as many of the exchanges you had with the people around you. Were you fully present or were there barriers or filters in place? Were you preoccupied or distracted? Many of us are subconsciously on guard when it comes to our communication with new people which can be exhausting. The defence barriers are ready to come up to protect our self-image at any time. Unless we have solid experience of feeling safe with others because we know them well, a certain amount of shadow boxing can go on when we interact. Do I have to defend my ego? How much can I show my vulnerability? If we choose to keep those barriers down we are more likely to have productive, honest and satisfying exchanges with those around us. Spending too much time sizing each other up is a waste of energy and ultimately takes us away from our sense of self.

We have a chance to stop, check in with ourselves and come from a positive, constructive place with everyone we meet. We can choose to pause and allow someone to pass, we can smile at the person who always presents a scowl to the world, we can pass a few pleasantries with the person who serves us at the supermarket. What impression do we want to give of ourselves? How do we want to represent our best intentions?

Today's exercise

Quality communication

Consider your interactions and quality of communication with the people around you – your family, friends and work colleagues. What inspired your choices today? Did you come from a place of compassion, integrity and positivity? Or were you fearful of being judged or criticised? Remember that you are in control of all you say and do. Is there anything you can do differently tomorrow to be more authentic when it comes to your interactions? How can you ensure that you stay constructive and honest around challenging individuals? As usual, reflect and record your thoughts in your journal.

Today's exercise: Quality communication

Notes:

Day 76

Stop!

Learning how to be still, to really be still and let life happen
– that stillness becomes a radiance.

Morgan Freeman

Today is a day off from the programme with no box to be ticked. A day without reflection, journaling, contemplation or a specific activity or goal. Spend time doing something that makes you happy and relaxed, whether it's a meal with your family, a country ramble and a pub lunch with friends, diving into a good book or ploughing your way through a box set of your favourite comedy show. Just make sure you factor in a belly laugh or two. Enjoy!

Today's exercise

Enjoy yourself!

Reviewing my goals in the context of others

If there is any one secret of success, it lies in the ability
to get the other person's point of view and see things from
his angle as well as your own.

Henry Ford

Today's exercise

SWIFT review

Go back to the SWIFT model and think about the goals you set
yourself in terms of the Focus and Task (Days 42 and 43). How
do these targets impact on those around you, both at home and
at work? Are you able to see how you can be more beneficial to
the people in your life if you achieve these goals? If they are
time-consuming tasks have you thought about how your commitments to your family, friends and colleagues can still be
accommodated? With that in mind, you may wish to modify or
give a new context to the goals you've identified.

Today's exercise: SWIFT review

Notes:

Exercises throughout this section ◇   Exercises throughout the book

Random acts of kindness   Wake up with gratitude
Invest in meaningful   and vision
relationships   Meditation
                                    Ask for help
                                  Tune into your body
                                  Review your goals
                             Be actively more supportive
                            Happiness for no good reason
                                  A little and often
                                   Write it down

Day 78

Sharing my reflections

Seek first to understand, then to be understood.

Stephen Covey

Today's exercise

Share your journey

Today, try to find someone you trust and have a supportive relationship with to discuss your thoughts and feelings, so that you have a witness for your journey. Are you discovering anything new about yourself? Are things being confirmed that you already knew? What is frustrating you or giving you difficulty? There may be things you'd like to check with someone, an idea or a perspective. Perhaps you are feeling uncomfortable in the light of changes that you realise need to be made. Take time to share your revelations and see what ideas and reactions the other person has.

Today's exercise: Share your journey

Notes:

Exercises throughout this section ◇   Exercises throughout the book

Random acts of kindness

Invest in meaningful
relationships

Wake up with gratitude
and vision

Meditation

Ask for help

Tune into your body

Review your goals

Be actively more supportive

Happiness for no good reason

A little and often

Write it down

Section 7

Complexity

Seeing the Bigger Picture

Revisiting my goals:
A rigorous assessment

Remember the two benefits of failure; first, if you do fail,
you learn what doesn't work; and second, the failure gives
you the opportunity to try a new approach.

Roger Von Oech

When we are repeatedly thwarted by the unexpected twists and turns of life we may feel that making concrete plans to reach our goals is pointlessly simplistic. This is understandable given all the variables that crop up as we journey towards the unknown. The old adage that life is what's happening while you're making other plans resonates. That doesn't mean to say that you should leave everything to chance, just in case things don't work out! After all, if you don't know where you are going, how will you recognise it when you get there?

The key is staying flexible and being willing to revise your aims and ideas given any changes to your circumstances. We need to keep alert to what we can have influence over and what is immutable in life. It's about striking a balance between what we would ideally like and what is feasible, given our reality.

It's also being prepared to fail – to try something and get it 'wrong'. It's only by investigating an option or putting an idea into action that we discover if it's worthwhile for us. That's why the SWIFT exercise is a practical rather than a theoretical model. We need to dive in and be prepared to get our hands dirty if we are to embed lasting, effective change. If we are afraid to fail then the very idea of things not going our way can become painful, especially if our failure is a public one (e.g. we don't succeed in setting up a business or a relationship doesn't work out). It's important to remember that the more adventurous and risk-taking we are, the more likely it is that we may trip up or be wrong-footed by our circumstances. But moving forward can mean following a less-than-straight path – we need to be clear about that before we embark on any new venture.

Today's exercise

Re-evaluation

It's worth spending time reviewing the SWIFT model (Day 35) and the focus and tasks you decided upon after consulting with others (Days 42 and 43). Having by now pinpointed the focus and embarked on the tasks, do they need modifying or clarifying? Perhaps you have realised that you need to be more specific about the timeline, or you may feel a need to restate your task or you are perhaps avoiding tackling a particular area that is the most challenging for you? Sometimes we kid ourselves that we are locking horns with an issue or an area of weakness when we aren't actually defining the true nature of it. Are you being honest with yourself? Go back to the reflections of your colleagues and friends when it came to feeding back on your strengths, weaknesses and areas for improvement. Does your task/tasks truly reflect these? Time to re-evaluate!

Today's exercise: Re-evaluation

Notes:

Exercises throughout this section ◇ Exercises throughout the book
Wake up with gratitude
and vision
Meditation
Ask for help
Tune into your body
Review your goals
Be actively more supportive
Happiness for no good reason
A little and often
Write it down

Day 80

Be a warrior, not a worrier

Everything will be alright in the end.
If it's not alright now, it's not the end!

Anon.

How many of us walk around with a head full of to-do
lists? Do you suffer from a vague sensation of guilt
because you can never fully address the relentless
number of tasks and chores that need to be achieved? For
many of us, our default position is low-level stress and anxiety – it fuels us through each day. The danger is that our focus
is therefore habitually narrow and self-referential, although
we may still feel a vague and dissatisfying sensation that there
are far more worthwhile things to engage with to improve our
well-being.

We've all heard the expression 'don't sweat the small stuff'.
What defines the small stuff varies from person to person.
Those petty, day-to-day details of bank charges, train delays,
silly misunderstandings, stressful office politics, car repairs
costing twice as much as we'd been quoted ... the list is endless.
Easy to say 'don't worry about it', of course, we hear you chorus.
But it's our attitude to the trivia that's key. How much priority do we give to complaining about it and suffering in the face
of it? If we're not careful, grumbling about our lot can become
our modus operandi. We fail to step back and see the people,
the blessings, the defining moments and positive aspects of our
lives that we should invest in for our growth.

It's not often that we get the luxury of being able to put everything into that bigger context, where the minor details fall away
and we can see our lives for what they really are. Sadly, it can
take a big shock – a bereavement, a tragedy that impacts on us
in an unexpected way – for everything to slam into focus and for

us to realise our petty concerns are just that: insubstantial, not worth wasting precious energy on.

Guess what? We have a choice – that word again! The way we see the world and what we beam into it as a result is the way we believe it actually is. If we are constantly bound up with worrying, or we don't trust people or we feel embittered about our relationships, what do you know, that's what we create. We project something and it is shown back to us on our own unique cinema screen. We become hostages to the fortune we've created – and if it's a negative, anxious one, life is very glass-half-empty.

Redirect your energy

How often do you consider the bigger questions? It's so tempting to drop down into the detail but getting perspective and asking yourself if you are truly living the life you want to live is vital for deep and lasting integrity and a sense of purpose. Are you spending enough time constructing positive, growthful relationships, tending to your well-being, following a meaningful path? Are you able to step back sufficiently to see where your life is heading, whatever crossroads you may be at? Can you lift your gaze away from the minutiae and invest in a meaningful future for yourself? Most of the time things take care of themselves in the long run – how many times have you said to yourself, 'I can't believe I worried so much about that, considering how it turned out ...'? Over the next few days, try to think of an area in your life where that precious energy can be redirected in a meaningful way.

Notes:

Day 81

Panning the camera back: Where am I currently heading?

If we don't change our direction,
we're likely to end up where we're going.

Anon.

Following on from yesterday, today's theme is about taking an eagle-eye perspective on our progress – looking at where we've come from and how the seeds were sown by the choices we made that led us to the current place in our lives. How does this information help us think about where we go next? Are you in the driving seat or are you clinging on to the bumper, a victim of circumstance?

Sometimes life can feel like a serious of accidents or happenstances – perhaps we found ourselves at the right time at the right place, we followed our gut or we just knew that a particular opportunity was a 'now or never' moment that had to be seized. Equally, we can look back and see no sort of pattern or plan; it may feel that we were buffeted by circumstances, went with the flow or pleased other people. All too often we can be swayed by what we think we ought to do or what is expected of us by our family, society, God (if we believe in one) and so on.

We can all look back and see other routes we could have taken that may have informed our lives differently. What's important is our ability to check in with the depths (that trusty inner compass) and see what the quiet and dignified voice within is encouraging us to do. Do you recognise that voice? Or is it drowned out by the monkey chatter?

We are often sold the lie that change is the preserve of the young; the malleable ones who are still sculpting their lives; the suggestible, the energetic, the naive. Sometimes it's just too difficult to accept the fact that we can make changes whenever and wherever we want to – however old we are or set in our ways. If we truly take that on board then life can sometimes feel a bit too challenging or risky. It may mean we have to drag ourselves out of a fur-lined rut and take responsibility in a new way. Sometimes we are called to make a change in our lives and we ignore it – but the thwarted expectation is still there, underneath all the chatter, the details and the excuses, and we feel a niggling sense of unfulfilment which can blight our happiness and day-to-day existence.

It's true that life is about now, about the present, about the only moment that we have any real control over – the one we are currently in. Life is constructed through the culmination of these many moments, like beads along a chain. If we can look back and see where we took charge of a moment, it can help us think about how to move forward from where we are with a sense of purpose and accountability – even if our choice doesn't work out the way we intended.

Today's exercise

Taking control

What decisions did you make in the past that were wise ones? Why were they wise? What did you gain or lose from those big decisions? According to your SWIFT answers, are you heading in the direction that is right for you? Are there any new ambitions appearing on your horizon? Sit with the quiet voice and see what it wants for you. Are you being true to it? Are there changes that you are putting off because they feel too fundamental or too effortful? How can you help yourself? Reach for your journal and record your thoughts.

Today's exercise: Taking control

Notes:

Day 82

Meditation: Change for life

There came a time when the risk to remain tight in the bud
was more painful than the risk it took to blossom.

Anaïs Nin

This Nin quote is a profound one. Staying in a situation or way of thinking that isn't constructive for us can be more endangering to our well-being than breaking out and venturing forth into the unknown, with all its scary newness. The sensation referred to yesterday of unfulfilment or dissatisfaction is a painful one that many of us learn to live with, like a tiny piece of grit in the bottom of your shoe. It's a dull ache and it can become a buffer that separates us from the present moment and sometimes from those around us; a deep distraction that disconnects us from making the most of now. Usually these feelings point towards the need for a shift in thinking or attitude; sometimes it's about having put off a big decision that is asking to be addressed – leaving a relationship, a job or a town. We tend to shy away from discomfort so these deep-seated feelings of dislocation stay under wraps and we stay stuck when we need to move on.

It's easy to talk about the value of making changes, to theorise and bandy the concept around. The importance of knowing we can be more accountable, more truly authentic by allowing ourselves more freedom of choice is a familiar one to most of us. We are of course able to intellectualise this, to consider the value of it, but fully integrating it is a different matter. If we live through the experience of making a change and creating a positive result we are more likely to recognise the opportunities in our lives when we need to step up to the plate again, and it won't feel so challenging. Taking a leap into the unknown takes a level of faith that can be hard to find, but experience and reality is always our guide. It helps to know too that what can feel monumentally huge in our imagination can be deconstructed and broken down into practical steps – we don't necessarily have to plunge off the edge of the cliff. But we do need to shine a torch on those difficult feelings as regularly as we dare.

Make embracing change a habitual reality

Give yourself twenty minutes and find a space where you can relax and be undisturbed. Get into a comfortable upright position and put your attention on the breath entering and leaving your body. Focus on the ebb and flow of inhalation and exhalation around your solar plexus. Enjoy the feeling of deep relaxation and allow any thoughts, ideas, opinions or voices to scud past your field of vision like clouds. Imagine you are gathering your straying thoughts and energies back into that relaxed centre; like casting a net to pull those fundamental parts of yourself back to that quiet and strong place.

Centre on one aspect that you would like to change or improve about yourself or your environment – perhaps it's part of your SWIFT plan. Allow any associated negative or destructive sensations that arise to come and go; try to stay detached. Instead, see yourself happy and relaxed having made that change or taken on that challenge. How does it feel? What has become stronger in you as a result of imagining it? Enjoy the sensations. Breathe them into your centre. Let them fuel you.

Today's exercise: Make embracing change a habitual reality

Notes:

Day 83

Charting my evolution: A timeline

Can you feel there is something in you that would rather be right than at peace?

Eckhart Tolle

Memories are an extraordinary phenomenon. They can feel as real and vivid as the present moment. They can also keep us stuck in old thought patterns and self-beliefs and, in that case, hinder personal development. These recollections are very subjective and are often shaped in a manner that supports the existing self-belief. This is particularly true when the viewpoint is expressed in a defined role such as 'victim', 'lone wolf', 'loser' and so on. Being stuck in such roles is a hindrance to us reacting intuitively and being mindful of the present moment, so everything that happens to us is filtered through the self-belief. In other words, we behave in line with our self-image. This behaviour, in turn, perpetuates and strengthens the self-belief and in this way creates a negative cycle.

Another more positive function of memories is to serve as constructive reminders of how far we have come in our personal evolution. By reflecting on how an old and discarded self-image used to make us behave, and analysing how differently we behave today, we are positively reinforcing our development.

Affirmative memories

Perhaps you would like to map this in your journal. Ask yourself the following questions:

- How do I nurture myself?

- How do I nurture my loved ones?

- How do I contribute positively to my surroundings?

Now go back to your past and ask yourself the same questions, thinking back one year, three years, seven years and so on, however long works for you. Reflect upon how you have changed in your behaviour as your personal evolution has taken place. Have you improved or fallen behind in nurturing yourself, your tribe and your surroundings?

Today's exercise: Affirmative memories

Notes:

Day 84

Focus on the present

The ego wants to want more than it wants to have.

Eckhart Tolle

Just as memories can keep us trapped in negative self-beliefs, so too can our ideas about the future. The role being played by the ego can dictate that only when certain things happen will we be happy. The 'victim' might think that only when he gets revenge on the 'perpetrator' will he be happy. The 'loser' thinks only when she has landed that coveted job, or met a certain kind of partner will she be happy. This projection into the future enhances the feeling of lack in the moment; since the future event hasn't taken place yet happiness can't be experienced until it does.

A healthy future focus is firmly based in the present. By being mindful of our behaviour today we are sowing the seeds of future experiences. By focusing on being present, calm and compassionate we will engage with people and experiences today that will lead to positive experiences to come. The present moment is the only one that is guaranteed, that actually exists. Everything else is in our minds, so only by controlling our present behaviour can we create the reality we want for ourselves.

Today's exercise

Focus on the present

Let go of the idea that you need to plan the future in order to be centred and content. You can do this by meditating on the idea that you are centred and content right now and realise this by staying in the mindset it perpetuates. It is by intensifying your experience of the present that you guarantee that all the future present moments will be as mindful and happy as this one. If you are currently undergoing something traumatic this may feel very difficult. That is OK. In that case, try to gently accept that the best thing you can do for yourself in this moment is to honestly accept your pain and by feeling it and working through it you will grow stronger and move through it.

Today's exercise: Focus on the present

Notes:

Day 85

Think big: A brand new personal challenge

Success is the sum of small efforts
repeated day in and day out.

Robert Collier

It is easy to become myopic when viewing life. Everyday events and challenges seem to take up all our available time and energy, yet there is often a desire for a better sense of direction and a greater purpose. We sometimes wonder how to find that resolve. Perhaps we feel powerless in the face of the enormity of time and events and wonder if we can truly impact on our lives.

As mentioned above, self-organising systems is a strain within modern sciences looking at the way systems grow and change. This theory presents an intriguing idea that when a system (e.g. society) is far from equilibrium, even a small change (such as one person's actions) can have an amplifying impact on the entire structure. This small change working its way into the system will be amplified when other parts of the system (i.e. other individuals) come into contact with it – like ripples on water expanding and affecting the entire surface of the pond.

Our individual impact is as significant as any other part of the system. Our responsibility is therefore our personal effect on the whole.

Think big

Think about how you can create space in your life to think big. What actions can you take to feel more participative and impactful? Do you have a cause or idea that you are particularly passionate about? What you can do to further that cause?

In your journal take a moment to reflect on what you are really passionate about. Put each idea or cause in the middle of a blank page. Then start to create a spider diagram or a mind-map, freely putting down ideas on how you can take action around the central issue. Let your inspiration guide you. Can you donate funds? Can you join an organisation? Do you need to inform yourself more about the issue? Can you start a blog?

Go back to your previous goal-setting exercises and see how you can start to include your idea as part of your concrete goals. Go back to SMART (Day 57) and make a timeline of action points ensuring that they are realistic and achievable. Take at least one action today!

Today's exercise: Think big

Notes:

Am I congruent?
Dealing with fragmentation

Only those who dare to fail greatly can ever achieve greatly.

Robert F. Kennedy

By being congruent we mean to what extent are you the sum of your parts. By this definition the short answer is you're not. No one is. So stop expecting congruency of yourself! Such a constant barrage of information and events exist that require constant reaction from us so congruency is hard to achieve. However, by applying rigorous analysis to our behaviour we can become more consistent in our approach and start to see what it is that throws us off balance. The more we do this, the better we will be at catching ourselves.

Consider this: the most successful people are better than average at failing. When they fail they accept that their aim was off, then they apply rigorous analysis to what they did wrong, learn from their mistakes and consequently improve their performance. Consistently.

Today's exercise

Learn from your mistakes

What do we consider to be the biggest mistake we've ever made? What did we learn from it? How can we move on from a sense of failure so that it doesn't stop us from trying something new again?

Today's exercise: Learn from your mistakes

Notes:

The madness of the ego, the majesty of the soul

The definition of insanity is doing the same thing over and over and expecting different results.

Rita Mae Brown

The ego defines itself by its separateness from other forms. It operates on historical information or experience, in the same way that the brain has preferred neural pathways to most efficiently achieve a certain task. The ego, by its definition of separateness, only knows itself. Change is the ultimate unknown and therefore a fearful idea to the ego. Change is to try something different to get a different result; however, that presupposes a transcendence of the fear of the unknown.

The trick is to start to sense this separateness and look for where it originates and how it sustains itself. Once we can do this we can sense the difference between the ego and the deeper consciousness, or soul. In this way the ego can continue to operate and get on with the business of doing, without us getting dragged into the dramas and emotional storms that accompany an unrestrained ego. Our deeper consciousness can just gently observe what the ego is getting up to and ensure no uncontrolled behaviours ensue.

The ego is revealed in our disproportionate emotional responses to events and people. An invaluable way to spot it is to look at what we dislike in others. Looking particularly closely at family members is interesting as they often provoke our earliest behavioural responses. The behaviours and traits they display that annoy us sometimes do so because we have the same egotistic traits and play the same roles. It is also useful to listen to how we talk about ourselves and others. When we describe behaviours that we dislike in others it can often be an indication of our ego playing out a role.

Mirror, mirror

Sit quietly with your journal and make a list of your closest family members and friends. Divide the page into two columns – likes and dislikes. Then go through the individuals one by one. Try not to over-think or let your own self-judgement get in the way. Remember, this is a private exercise for you and is not designed to be shared with anyone, so be honest with yourself.

Once you've finished, reflect quietly on your findings and ask yourself if they mirror back characteristics you have within you. Take note of the traits you found that you would like to change in yourself and work that into your personal development practice.

Today's exercise: Mirror, mirror

Notes:

Exercises throughout this section ◇ Exercises throughout the book
Redirect your energy   Wake up with gratitude
and vision
Meditation
Ask for help
Tune into your body
Review your goals
Be actively more supportive
Happiness for no good reason
A little and often
Write it down

Living like it's your last day

Twenty years from now you will be more disappointed by the things that you didn't do than by the ones you did do.

Mark Twain

As far as we know, there is nothing we can do about the passage of time. Life will progress and there is no way of knowing when it will end. We have no control over the *quantity* of time available to us; the *quality* of our time however is where we do have some influence.

There is perhaps an over-reliance on activity or 'doing' as a means to happiness, and a corresponding under-appreciation of the importance of our mindset when going into an activity. Although it is no doubt wonderful to fill our lives with exciting activities, it's important to realise that our mindset will either imbue the situation with profound meaning or make it feel superficial and dissatisfying. If we are in the middle of a thrilling event, say getting married, but we are preoccupied with whether the organisation is good enough and if it will impress the future in-laws, we will certainly not be having the most enjoyable day of our life. We will be stressed and worried. On the other hand, we might feel peaceful during a quiet walk through a forest. On the surface that might not sound like an exhilarating experience – but between the two, when are we most content? The point is that any experience can be fantastic with a mindset of presence, gratitude and wonderment at the uniqueness of that moment. It is not the event itself which dictates how we feel about it. The activity can only ever give us an expectation; it is our interaction with it that will determine how we eventually feel about it.

Taking time to create a positive mindset will help us realise just how precious life is. It will help us to wipe the diary clean of mindless doing and instead fill our time with what is truly important to us.

Live more truthfully

If this were your last day, would you be happy and content and ready to go? Have you filled today with honesty, love and presence or mindless judgement, superficiality and distractions?

In your morning meditation, think about all the things you do and have in your life that make you happy. What is truly important to you? If this really was your last day, what would you do? Who would you call? What would you say? Which wounds need healing? Who do you truly love and do they know you feel that way? What personal qualities are genuinely important to you and are you living them, working on them and looking for them in others? Make a vow to start living more truthfully, which means taking actions to answer the questions above. Look for ways to insert honesty, love and integrity into everything you do and all your relationships. Stop judging. Stop wasting time on distractions.

Exercises throughout this section ◇	Exercises throughout the book
Redirect your energy	Wake up with gratitude and vision
	Meditation
	Ask for help
	Tune into your body
	Review your goals
	Be actively more supportive
	Happiness for no good reason
	A little and often
	Write it down
	Live more truthfully

Stop!

*If you think you are so enlightened,
go spend a week with your parents.*

Ram Dass

To stop judging and to start to forgive is a wonderful experience – it gives us freedom to move forward without being weighed down by the past. Instead of hanging on to regret and a sense of missed opportunities, how about forgiving yourself and accepting that you acted to the best of your capability with the knowledge you had at the time, as did everyone else?

The past is not a finite and absolute entity, it is entirely subjective. The way we experience our memories of the past is an amalgamation of several things: physical activity, how we valued the situation at that time, how we and others have since described the events and how the descriptions best serve us in the present. Put another way, do we gain anything by painting a certain picture of a past event in order to solicit certain emotional responses from somebody today? Consider also that everyone else is stuck on the same carousel. They are also warping their recollections and judging past events using today's knowledge. Surely they too could be forgiven for being as smart or as foolish as we are?

Start forgiving

Sit down in a relaxed position. Now think in turn about all the people in your life that you have some conflict with. Imagine they are sitting there in front of you. Now remember that they too are navigating their way through life just as much as you are and they might also get it wrong. Focus on their good qualities. Remind yourself that they are someone's daughter/son, friend, parent, colleague and so on, and are worthy of love and respect just as you are.

Now remind yourself that you may also have acted inconsiderately towards them and that you would like their forgiveness. Finally imagine that you both embrace and with a big smile say you forgive each other.

You can do this exercise as many times as you like. It is very gentle and profound. It may also increase tolerance towards strangers as you remind yourself that they are equally worthy of your love and respect.

As a true challenge to yourself, next time you are stuck on public transport or in transit somewhere and you feel your blood starting to boil, take a deep breath and remind yourself of this meditation exercise. Imagine that you are extending your acceptance and forgiveness to everyone in your environment and that you are asking for theirs in return.

Notes:

Exercises throughout this section ◇ Exercises throughout the book
Redirect your energy Wake up with gratitude
Start forgiving and vision
Meditation
Ask for help
Tune into your body
Review your goals
Be actively more supportive
Happiness for no good reason
A little and often
Write it down
Live more truthfully

Day 90

Mind-map my journey

*I am always doing things I can't do –
that's how I get to do them.*

Pablo Picasso

Have you ever done a mind-map or spider diagram? You may have attempted one already in an earlier exercises (Days 60 and 85). They can be fun, especially if you are a doodler or a visual–spatial learner. Although there are all sorts of rules on how to do them correctly (Google it and you will see), the most important aspect is the creativity and freedom, as you allow your thoughts to move non-linearly.

The idea is to put a word in the middle of the page and then start in all directions, drawing arrows, thought bubbles, pictures and so on that you associate with this word. Be free to put down whatever comes to mind. Use multiple coloured pens too to inspire you further; some people believe colours have different emotional 'vibrations' attached to them, so this can help to manifest a certain thought.

We can highly recommend this process whenever you are at the beginning of a new phase or project or when you feel stuck in some way and need inspiration to strike.

Today's exercise

Mind-map

Bring out several pieces of blank paper and coloured pens. Start by putting a word in the middle of the page. It can be anything you like – for example, a project you are working on, a personal trait you want to develop, a person or maybe simply 'my life'. Start the process as described above, drawing lines extending out from the central idea and writing down any thoughts that come to mind that you associate with the word. It can include dates, pictures, goals, people, emotions, music, films and so on. The point is to let your mind freely associate with the word and not judge what comes out. You may be surprised at some of the ideas. You may also find solutions to a conundrum that has until now appeared unsolvable. When you feel content with the first word, take out another sheet of paper and put a different word in the middle as the key idea and start the process again.

Today's exercise: Mind-map

Notes:

Exercises throughout this section ◇   Exercises throughout the book
Redirect your energy   Wake up with gratitude
Start forgiving   and vision
                                               Meditation
                                              Ask for help
                                        Tune into your body
                                         Review your goals
                                   Be actively more supportive
                                  Happiness for no good reason
                                        A little and often
                                         Write it down
                                       Live more truthfully

Day 91

Cause and effect and how we create our own reality

The world is only a potential and not present
without me or you to observe it.

Fred Allen Wolf

There exists a fairly well known phenomenon called cause and effect. Reality is often perceived as absolute, tangible fact. However, everything we experience from the outside is entirely subjective because we filter these experiences through the five senses. However, our hearing, sight, touch, smell and taste mechanisms are not an exact replica of anyone else's, so it is impossible to create a set of absolute versions of a sensory experience. The intake of information will shape our view of the world and inform our unique system of how to react. On top of the biological differences from person to person, this information is also filtered through the entire make-up of who we are (personality, background, tendencies, conditioning, etc.), thereby creating a unique experience.

There is currently an overemphasis on the sense of sight ('seeing is believing'), although Daniel Levitin has shown that sight is in fact an amalgamation of the visual imprint on the retina and the mind's rapid processing of that image. In other words, the brain instantly scans for recorded memories of similarly received information to categorise and interpret it in various ways to help us make sense of what we just saw. Obviously, no human being has got a complete record of everything there is to see, so how can there be a fixed version or interpretation of what reality is? This is exactly why people who are shown identical images, or who were present at the same event, will recount vastly different versions of what they saw because what they 'saw' draws on their unique memory bank.

Let's take this a step further. If everything we experience is subjective – unique to our version of reality – then it follows that our experience actually originates inside and not outside. There is no 'outside' that is independent from our internal process. It then follows that if we are the originator of our experiences, we can also control them or at least impact on them. This shifts the sense of control from the outside to the inside and empowers us in the realisation that we do have influence over how we feel about things. We become more proactive rather than reactive.

If this theory is to be believed, there is no agreed version of reality, no *absolute* reality. Once we have gone through the exercise of exposing our belief system, we can turn it around and consider how we can influence the outside to suit the inside. We may not necessarily alter external events but we can change the way we perceive and interpret them, and consequently modify our emotional responses in relation to the experience. Add to this the idea that a given cause can only produce a given effect (this is in essence what cause and effect means). Now when we get a deeper understanding of what the cause of our experience really is (i.e. ourselves) we will start to be 'wisely selfish' (to quote the Dalai Lama) and create the effect we want. We can work at achieving a positive internal state since we know that it will create a positive external experience. We 'see' what we want to see. We are now creating our own reality.

Today's exercise

Have a laugh

Confused? Then it's probably time to have a good laugh. Maybe it's all a huge cosmic joke – either way, laughing will make you feel better! Sit comfortably and start to laugh out loud as long and as heartily as you want. Recall a particularly funny memory or just make funny faces, slap your knees, get up and jump

---

around. Let it rumble through your tummy and up through your vocal cords and out into space. Let it just flow. Relax and feel a warm glow inside.

Today's exercise: Have a laugh

Notes:

Section 8

Holistic

An Existential Outlook

Day 92

'What is in the one, is in the whole'

When we concentrate on individual moments or fragments of experience, we see only chaos. But if we stand back and look at what is taking shape, we see order.

Margaret Wheatley

Where do you end and I begin? At the skin? Do our shared feelings and ideas belong to you or me? Where do we draw the line? Do we exist outside of our relationship to one another and everyone else? Who is there to observe whether we do or not? Can we define life separately from everything we observe around us? Can you take yourself out of 'life' and observe it as a discrete idea? Can you define life without talking about the parts that make up life such as you, me, animals, trees, ideas and concepts? Can you define me without acknowledging that I am part of life?

Today's exercise

Eliminate separateness

Search out and seek to eliminate any feelings of isolation or separateness between yourself and others; yourself and life. Meditate on the idea that what is in the one is in the whole.

Today's exercise: Eliminate separateness

Notes:

Day 93

Practising gratitude

Don't sow a lemon seed and expect an orange tree.

Kabbalistic proverb

For the philosophical among you, what comes first: the question or the answer? What if it's the answer? If we accept this, then we accept that we already have all the answers to all our questions. We will not get the answer though before we ask the right question – because that provides the focus. In other words, we do the action first, knowing that we already have the reward. We feel the gratitude for what we will receive because we have already received it.

Looking at the proverb above, the point is that we need to nurture our seeds and make sure we sow the right ones. The way to know which are the right ones is to be sure what trees they will grow into. Put the questioning not into why a lemon seed won't grow into an orange tree but into which type of lemon tree you want. Then nurture that, be grateful for your lemon tree and don't worry about not having an orange one!

Today's exercise

Ask yourself for guidance

Prepare as you learnt on Day 1 for the evening gratitude exercise. Once you have exhausted your list and feel in a state of relaxation and gratitude, meditate on the areas of your life you would like some guidance on. Imagine that you are having a conversation with the universe/your inner self/your heart or whichever image you use to represent your deeper consciousness. Now ask to receive an answer to your question overnight. Make sure you state the question clearly and in a positive way. For example, if you are struggling in your relationship don't ask, 'How can I stop being so selfish?' Instead ask, 'How can I be more loving and understanding towards my partner?' The reason for this is that when you state a question positively it starts to become an affirmation – you are already setting the intention. You are helping your mind to look for a solution, so it is important that you are asking for positive and proactive answers and actions.

Tomorrow when you wake up, immediately remind yourself of what your question was and see if any ideas come to mind. Write down any dreams you remember as they can hold vital clues that may not be immediately obvious but make sense when later reviewed. This can take a few attempts but you will soon find just how productive you are during your sleep!

Notes:

Exercises throughout this section ◇
Ask yourself for guidance

Exercises throughout the book
Wake up with gratitude
and vision
Meditation
Ask for help
Tune into your body
Review your goals
Be actively more supportive
Happiness for no good reason
A little and often
Write it down
Live more truthfully

Day 94

Meditation: Observing my new reality

Smile, breathe and go slowly.

Thich Nhat Hanh

Now we are ready to start practising meditation in action. This is the state of mindfulness – of gently being present in the moment and staying aware of our feelings and actions. We have a calm hold over our emotional responses; we are not reactive to external events and other people's behaviour. We are loving and we are developing an accepting attitude towards everyone. At this point, it is worth looking for motivational sources to help us stay in a positive state.

Inspiration provides wonderful positive energy and elation that makes us want to go out into the world and create new ideas, relationships and projects. Just as negative energy can create stumbling blocks in the way it shuts us down and blocks us from seeing clearly, so inspiration creates positive energy which acts like a bulldozer pushing problems out of the way. It unlocks the solutions lying dormant within the issue. The more positive energy you feel the higher your 'vibration' or openness; the greater the openness the more positive the energy you experience will be.

We will now start to look for more ways of extending kindness to people in our lives, for opportunities to be helpful and selfless to strangers. This might be donating more to charities, volunteering or in other ways lending support to organisations or individuals.

Perform an act of kindness

This exercise takes you back to your journal. Start making notes about what makes you feel inspired and pledge to increase your exposure to these things, be it art, people, travel, being outdoors, good food, sports, politics, animals and so on. The point is to find out what is unique to you and to use this to help others.

Let's go back to the random acts of kindness exercise (Day 69). Perform at least one act of kindness every day this week.

Notes:

Exercises throughout this section ◇

Ask yourself for guidance
Perform an act of kindness

Exercises throughout the book

Wake up with gratitude and vision
Meditation
Ask for help
Tune into your body
Review your goals
Be actively more supportive
Happiness for no good reason
A little and often
Write it down
Live more truthfully

Day 95

Is this it?

The unexamined life is not worth living.

Socrates

Spirituality and religion are often mistaken for the same thing. Religion can be seen as a human-constructed system including rituals, ethics, morals and codes of conduct. It also offers a series of ideas of what 'God' is. These ideas fall under belief as opposed to fact as there is no scientific proof, not yet at least, that confirms the existence of God. Religion may or may not contain spirituality and the practitioners of a faith may be more or less in tune with their spirituality than others, albeit they still practise the rituals of their religion.

Spirituality, on the other hand, can be defined as an individual's ability and need for a deeper understanding of the meaning of life, which may include existential questions, the exploration of alternative realities and planes of existence and a sense of connectedness to a greater whole. This is a naturally occurring human trait and as such is integral to the pursuit of profound knowledge and wisdom. A person can be deeply spiritual without practising any form of organised religion.

Any muscle that gets trained becomes stronger, including our 'mental muscles'. We can effectively train ourselves in all areas of life and improve our mastery, including being spiritual and intuitive. In this book there are several practical exercises aimed at working our mental muscles. When we do these exercises do we actually 'know' what happens and where the change comes from? Is our belief system important in this process? If we experience growth and even a sense of transcendence, where does that originate? Is it ourselves or is there an intervention by some divine principle?

What we 'know' is that we are experiencing a change in our perception of reality. We feel differently. What or who is the originator of that change? Is it a Creator who removes an old memory or emotion? Do emotions stay in the body or is it the psyche that wants to be rid of negative thought patterns? Then what is the 'psyche'? If we are part of this holistic system called life, creation and so on, is not our psyche as much the Creator as any other external force? If the result is positive, does it matter?

The process of asking these questions and exploring the answers can be extremely fulfilling. Your personal belief system is important as it can either help or hinder you to experience change, so it is essential that it supports you in the continued growth of your spiritual muscles.

Today's exercise

Let go of your pain

Prepare your morning meditation. When you have reached a sense of calm observation of the breath do the following visualisation. Imagine that you have in front of you a ring of light. In that ring you are going to put all your pain. Ask yourself what pains you on a physical level in relation to your body; on an emotional level in terms of your relationships; an intellectual level in relation to your achievements; and an intuitive/spiritual level connected to your place in the greater scheme of things. Be very honest with yourself and do not judge what comes out. Place every one of those pains in the ring.

Once you have reviewed your life on these different levels and all your pain has been identified and put in the ring, imagine now that it is no longer a part of you and cannot influence you. All your pain is contained within the ring. Repeat to yourself: 'I am not my pain'. Imagine that you are empowered, centred and unaffected by the pain; you are complete and perfect just as you are. When you are ready, let the vision dissolve. Take a moment

---

to come back to yourself in the present and feel grateful for this moment of cleansing.

Today's exercise: Let go of your pain

Notes:

Day 96

Being guided by
my inner compass

You become most powerful in whatever you do if the action
is performed for its own sake rather than as a means to
protect, enhance, or conform to your role identity.

Eckhart Tolle

In this book we have suggested activities such as visualising, planning, goal-setting, taking action, dreaming big and being proactive. All of these are essential parts of the process of deepening our self-knowledge and clearing out entrenched and often limiting self-beliefs. Slowly and purposefully we are peeling off the layers between our outer and inner selves, between our compass and our purpose. Once this process has been undertaken we arrive at the point of finding our inner guide – our deep, true and authentic self. When we are in touch with that part of ourselves there is no longer any need for plans, goals and wants. We can trust that we will be steered in the moment to make the correct decisions. We can trust that we are exactly as we should be. This inner voice is always there; louder when we are calm and at peace, softer when we get caught up in life's events. Now we have a process we can revisit when our self needs strengthening. Now we have the courage to let go of the need for wanting and just trust.

Let go of your goals

Prepare your morning meditation. When you have reached a sense of calm observation of the breath do the following visualisation. As with yesterday, imagine that you have in front of you a ring of light. In that ring you are going to put every plan, goal or expectation that you have. Ask yourself what you want to achieve on the physical level in relation to your body, emotionally and intellectually as well as intuitively/spiritually. Visualise placing every one of those goals in the ring. Be very honest with yourself and do not judge what comes out.

Once you have reviewed your life on these different planes and all your desires and goals have been put in the ring, imagine they are no longer a part of you, they can no longer influence you. They are contained within the circle. Repeat to yourself: 'I am not my achievements'. Imagine that you are empowered, centred and unaffected by the need to achieve anything; you are complete and perfect just as you are. When you are ready, let the vision dissolve. Take a moment to come back to yourself and feel grateful for this moment of cleansing.

Today's exercise: Let go of your goals

Notes:

Day 97

Informing my actions with integrity

It is never too late to be what you might have been.

George Eliot

Yesterday we visualised what it's like to let go of the need for achievement. Does this mean we become complacent and careless about what happens to us? Far from it. When we let go of the compulsive need for achievement we can look at what we do with greater reassurance that our choices are well informed by what our deeper sense of truth and self guides us to do.

We started this book by stating that love is the most important element of life. This is not romantic love, but rather the love and compassion for all things animate or inanimate. Yesterday's exercise brought us closer to a deeper sense of love and acceptance of our inner selves. Now let's extend that to everyone and everything, and see if we can inform our every action with love and integrity.

Today's exercise

Reassess your goals

Informed by yesterday's experience of letting go of your need to achieve, go back and review your goals in your journal. Ask yourself the following questions:

● Do I really need to achieve this to be happy?

- Are these goals serving the highest good of all concerned (my family and friends) or are they a reflection of my need for achievement?

- Is there a more loving way to go about these achievements?

- What can I do to help others achieve their full potential?

- How can I be more loving?

Ask yourself what your new goals are in four areas: spiritual, mental, emotional and physical. Write them out in your journal including anything that comes to mind – this is a free association exercise.

Once you have written them down, take each one in turn and think about how you can turn your dream into a concrete goal that you can take actions to achieve. Compare them to each other, one by one, and decide which are the most important to you at this point in time. This will help you to decide an order of priority.

Then take each goal in turn and break it down according to the structure described on Day 43.

Today's exercise: Reassess your goals

Notes:

Day 98

How can I be of unconditional service?

Who could have wished for more?

Stephen Hawking

There is something enormously freeing in surrendering – letting go of expectations and trusting that everything is just as it should be. The word 'surrender' means to give back. It can be very difficult, however, to maintain that sense of surrender as the ever-active mind/ego immediately wants to be in control. In the moment of surrender we are relinquishing the need to be in control and in charge; we accept and trust the outcome whatever it may be. To surrender does not mean abandonment of personal responsibility; it means an acceptance of the now as the only certainty there is, the only thing we can focus on.

Today's exercise

Let go of your control

After you have done your evening gratitude practice, imagine you are in a deep, dark, safe place – maybe like that childhood hide-out you used to build under your bed or in the garden. You could also imagine you have been transported back to the primordial point or centre of the universe. Once you feel enveloped by a sense of absolute safety and security, say out loud or in your head, 'I surrender unconditionally'. Repeat this mantra until you feel a deep sense of peace. Then let the vision/sense dissolve gently.

Today's exercise: Let go of your control

Notes:

Stop!

You can conquer almost any fear if you will only make up your mind to do so. For, remember, fear doesn't exist anywhere except in the mind.

Dale Carnegie

From an early age we learn that certain things are dangerous and that we will hurt ourselves if we go near them. These are fears that can be perceived by the senses – heat, height, sharp edges and so on – that are necessary for survival in the physical plane. In tandem with the formation of the ego there develops a growing sense of separation from others and the environment. This is a natural development of the ego as it represents the part of us which is the 'self' or the 'I', which is by definition separate from others and our environment. However, the by-product of the formation of the ego is the creation of fears like loneliness and rejection. This is because there is a conflict with our deeper consciousness which knows it is entirely connected to everything else. The ego is consequently incomplete in its very nature of separateness.

The fears created by ego formation are intangible as they sit outside of the world of the senses and therefore feel more elusive. Yet they can have debilitating effects on our life choices. As with all aspects of personal growth the starting point is always to honestly admit to any issues or fears. Pretending that we don't is just a trick of the ego which will only make them grow; if we don't recognise a fear, how can we work on it and diffuse its power over us?

Let go of your fear

Prepare your morning meditation. When you have reached a sense of calm observation of the breath, do the following visualisation. Once more imagine that you have in front of you a ring of light. In that ring you are going to put every fear that you have. Ask yourself what you are afraid of on the physical level in relation to your body, on an emotional and intellectual level and intuitively/spiritually, and visualise placing every one of those fears in the ring. Be very honest with yourself and do not judge what comes out.

Once you have reviewed your life on these different levels and all the fears have been put in the ring, imagine they are no longer a part of you, they can no longer influence you. They are contained within the ring. Repeat to yourself, 'I am not my fears'. Imagine that you are empowered, centred and unaffected by these fears. When you are ready let the vision dissolve. Take a moment to come back to yourself and feel grateful for this moment of cleansing.

This is a very powerful exercise that we would recommend you try again and again and again. Fears creep up on us and new ones will come in to take the place of the old ones, but you now hold a powerful tool to deal with them, so they will have a diminishing power over you.

Today's exercise: Let go of your fear

Notes:

Day 100

Celebrate my achievements with others

A day without laughter is a wasted day.

Anon.

Joy somehow grows when it is shared. The first thing we want to do when something wonderful happens to us is to share it with our loved ones. Working your way through this book is a fantastic achievement. You have truly honoured your own journey and hopefully come a long way. You are experiencing what it is like to go beyond what you perhaps thought possible and are stretching your boundaries. That joy now needs to be spread so it can grow and flow and inspire others!

Today's exercise

All we need is love

Think about somebody you love very dearly. Consider how you behave towards that person, the love and respect you inject into that relationship. Today you will imagine that you love everyone you meet just as much. You will inject the same amount of love and respect into every single interaction, whether it's someone you know or a stranger. Everyone you meet is someone's relative, someone's best friend, loved and treasured. Imagine he or she is one of your loved and treasured people. Do your best to share the joy with them.

Today's exercise: All we need is love

Notes:

Day 101

Look forward ...
to the next 101 days!

*When you recognise that the present moment is always
already the case and therefore inevitable, you can bring an
uncompromising inner 'yes' to it and so not only create no
further unhappiness, but, with inner resistance gone, find
yourself empowered by Life itself.*

Eckhart Tolle

Do you remember what your thoughts were at the outset of this journey when you first picked up this book? Did you have any clear ideas of where you wanted to go or what you wanted to achieve? Or were you just curious? Now that you are at the end of this 101-day process, are you where you expected to be?

Let this end inspire the beginning of your next 101 days. No doubt a rest will be needed as you let everything settle in and find its new home. Allow yourself to let go completely of all the last few months work and trust that the effect is there on a deeper level. Then, when you are ready, pick up this book again. This might be days, months or even years from today. The magic is that to reapply these ideas and exercises is never a repetition of work already completed. Instead you will find new levels to work on, even with seemingly the same issues. The life experience that will happen between now and when you start your next 101-day process will help you uncover new clues to the game of life and bring new information to light. You may want to put a marker in the sand today, but there truly is no end and no beginning. There is only the present moment, here and now.

Today

I will take

the

first steps

on

my new journey ...

About the Coral Collective

The Coral Collective delivers top-class consultancy with a dynamic difference – we guarantee uniquely creative and energised training experiences, delivered by an experienced team of communication experts, all with an arts background. Our values-based methods are always intellectually sound, spirited and innovative, yet ultimately sustainable.

The Coral Collective partners – Roy Leighton, Emma Kilbey and Kristina Bill – visit commercial and educational environments alongside trusted colleagues, focusing on personal and group evolution, change management and effective communication. We have an impressive track record in both the public and private sectors and the positive impact of our initial interventions has always led to either referrals or repeat business.

For further information please visit www.wearecoral.com

Roy Leighton

Roy has been working in value-based areas in education, the arts and business environments in the UK and internationally for over twenty-five years. He has written books on creativity, learning, parenting, leadership and confidence. His areas of expertise are many and varied – from providing inspiring and stimulating keynote speeches, whole day conferences and workshops and sustainable programmes that run for weeks and years, and on rare occasions, possibly lifetimes.

Emma Kilbey

From commercial values-based training programmes to transformational educational interventions, Emma strikes an inspiring balance between intellectual rigour, practical application, creativity and intuition. Originally trained as a journalist, she co-runs a successful theatre company and is also an actress, director, scriptwriter, diversity trainer and occasional cabaret crooner. A professional enthusiast, she gets a big buzz from truffling out people's uniqueness.

Kristina Bill

Kristina is one of the founding partners of the Coral Collective alongside Roy and Emma. She divides her time between the consultancy and her career as a recording artist and performer (www.kristinabill.com). She holds a Bachelor of Commerce, High Honours from Concordia University, Montreal, Canada and has further qualifications in performing arts, life coaching and fitness training. She has good working French and is fluent in her native Swedish.

Bibliography

Bowkett, S., Harding, T., Lee, T. and Leighton, R. (2008). *Happy Families: Insights into the Art of Parenting*. London: Network Continuum.

Bowkett, S., Lee, T., Harding, T. and Leighton, R. (2007). *Success in the Creative Classroom: Using Enjoyment to Promote Excellence*. London: Network Continuum.

Cameron, J. (1995). *The Artist's Way*. London: Pan Books.

Cartwright, T. J. (1991). 'Planning and Chaos Theory', *Journal of the American Planning Association* 57: 44–56.

Garner, L. (2004). *Everything I've Ever Done That Worked*. London: Hay House.

Graves, C.W. (1971). 'Seminar on Levels of Human Existence'. Paper presented at the Washington School of Psychiatry, Washington, DC, 16 October 1971. Available as *Clare W. Graves: Levels of Human Existence*, ed. W. R. Lee, C. Cowan and N. Todorovec. Santa Barbara, CA: ECLET Publishing.

Levitin, D. (2008). *This is Your Brain on Music: Understanding a Human Obsession*. London: Atlantic Books.

Luskin, F. (2003). *Forgive for Good: A Proven Prescription for Health and Happiness*. New York: HarperCollins.

Myss, C. (1997). *Anatomy of the Spirit: The Seven Stages of Power and Healing*. London: Bantam Press.

Peters, T. (1992). *Liberation Management: Necessary Disorganisation for the Nanosecond Nineties*. London: Pan Books.

Reid, D. (2003). *The Tao of Detox: The Natural Way to Purify Your Body for Health and Longevity*. London: Simon & Schuster.

Wheatley, M. (1999). *Leadership and the New Science: Discovering Order in a Chaotic World*. San Francisco, CA: Berrett-Koehler.

Index of exercises